PARKING LAW

PARKING LAW

CHARLES BRANDRETH
Solicitor

With a Foreword by
Sir Robert Mark
Commissioner of Police of the Metropolis

David & Charles
Newton Abbot London
North Pomfret (VT) Vancouver

ISBN 0 7153 7376 5
Library of Congress Catalog Card Number 76–58792

Set in 11 on 13pt Baskerville
and printed in Great Britain
by Redwood Burn Limited
for David & Charles (Publishers) Limited
Brunel House   Newton Abbot   Devon

Published in the United States of America
by David & Charles Inc
North Pomfret   Vermont 05053   USA

Published in Canada
by Douglas David & Charles Limited
1875 Welch Street   North Vancouver   BC

FOREWORD

I have known Charles Brandreth now for fifteen years and have marvelled at his patience and good humour in dealing with probably the most frustrating of all aspects of law, the control of the motorist.

There is an old military adage that you should never give an order that you cannot enforce. Parking laws have always been a classic example of the disregard of that principle. Lack of vision, failure to understand the practicalities of enforcement, moral cowardice or political expediency—or perhaps a combination of all four—have resulted in systems of parking control in urban areas that are unnecessarily wasteful of both money and manpower, socially unjust and predictably ineffective. Those who have framed our parking laws have never appreciated that drivers generally—even though they amount to three-fifths of the electorate—prefer clear and strong measures fairly administered to weak and ineffective ones dominated either by the ability to cheat or to pay more than the next man for an unfair share of parking space.

The problem has been tackled all the more ineffectively because of divided responsibility for planning, legislation and enforcement. Even now, measures to control the motorist (whether by parking zones or bus lanes) proliferate without any prospect of effective, fair, or uniform enforcement. And no-one seems to have thought of relating this continually expanding process to the willingness or unwillingness of the Courts to support it.

Motoring laws are now an almost indescribable mass of muddle and frustration from which for the first time there is to be seen, in the advent of owner liability, a faint glimmer of hope that reason is beginning to emerge. Sooner or later the realisation must come that the clearer the prohibition or regulation, the greater the certainty of conviction, the less will be the need for heavier penalties or additional manpower. Even more helpful would be the exclusion from the criminal law proper of minor motoring offences, allowing the extension of a thereby more acceptable though necessarily more arbitrary fixed penalty system.

However, the book demonstrates happily that Charles Brandreth's attempts to alleviate the suffering of past generations of motorists and his obvious concern for their future wellbeing have not affected the tolerance, the common sense and gentle wit that in his long association with the AA and with BBC's 'Motoring and the Motorist' have gained him so many friends and admirers, amongst whom I feel privileged to be included.

Robert Mark
Commissioner of Police of the Metropolis

Every unauthorised obstruction of a highway to the annoyance of the King's subjects is an indictable offence . . . No one can make a stableyard of the King's Highway.

Lord Ellenborough C J in R v Cross (1812), 3 Campbell's Reports

---

We recommend that the law be reviewed simplified and modernised so that any driver will know where he may and may not park his vehicle without committing an offence.

Final Report of the Royal Commission on the Police (1962)

Traffic wardens are not in general the pin-ups of the populace. They have frequently exasperating irritating and sometimes odious duties to perform, but they are duties which in the public interest have to be discharged and those who find the discharge of a warden's duty personally inconvenient must just put up with it. The duties are imposed for the benefit of the public at large.

Lord Justice Edmund Davies in R v Waclawski (1972), Court of Appeal (Criminal Division).

Advisory Service

Motoring organizations offer their members what amounts to a free diagnostic check-up on any parking ticket. It is part of their legal services. The member complains of unfair treatment. He has argued his case unsuccessfully and he needs advice.

There is a pseudo-medical approach to every ticket problem. The member is the patient. He feels sore. He presents the evidence, the 'blister', incurred under circumstances which he feels did not justify the penalty. Every ticket has its case history for which there is always a precedent, held in the archives of the legal adviser. The motoring organization (or **MO**) is concerned with diagnosis and prognosis. Not all blisters are malignant. They may respond to treatment.

Cases suitable for treatment are those which concern genuine loading or unloading, collecting or delivering, picking up and setting down, cases where the vehicle was left unattended. There will be numerous complaints also over faulty ticket machines and out of order parking meters, arguments over permits, alleged defective traffic signs. And there will be innumerable emergencies, breakdowns and compassionate cases generally. All require patient investigation. A local inspection by Highways and Traffic may be

9

required. The prognosis is bad in the majority of cases. But a proportion are diagnosed as worthy of representation and the experience is that up to 50 per cent of those referred for consideration result to the member's satisfaction. Payment is excused.

Not every ticket holder has a sympathetic MO. Most prefer DIY treatment, and many simply ignore the 'blister' until within the statutory period of six months it afflicts the registered owner. The consequences of ignoring the final offer to pay up 'or else' can be most unpleasant. An inquest on a ticket is one thing but a post mortem on a summons is quite another. Conservative treatment is always preferable to surgery. Magistrates who operate on parking offenders can be butchers. 'Arbitrate, don't litigate' is usually the best advice on every ticket problem.

Arrests

The number of people who manage to get themselves arrested following a parking incident is quite remarkable. Home Office statistics show that on average upwards of 300 parking offenders appear *in the dock* each year. They are arrested for meter zone offences, for dangerous parking, for obstruction, for failure to park on the nearside after dark, for stopping on a clearway and quite simply for 'other offences against waiting restrictions'.

The figures are remarkable when you consider that the only parking offence which of itself is arrestable is 'wilful obstruction':

> If a person without lawful authority or excuse in any way wilfully obstructs the free passage along a highway, he shall be guilty of an offence, and a constable may arrest without warrant any person whom he sees committing the offence. (s.121 Highways Act 1959).

'Wilful obstruction' really speaks for itself. The reported cases concern obstinate vendors of hot dogs and ice cream merchants. It is also invoked against difficult chauffeurs, those for example who block the traffic as they circle Covent Garden

Opera House, Bow Street police station being so handy.

But police also have powers of arrest in their ancient powers to suppress street nuisances—under the Metropolitan Police Act 1839 and the Town Police Clauses Act of 1847:

Every person who in any street to the obstruction annoyance or danger of the residents or passengers commits any of the following offences shall be liable to a penalty not exceeding £20 . . . and any constable shall take into custody, without warrant, and forthwith convey before a justice, any person who within his view, commits any such offence viz:
(inter alia) Every person who causes any public carriage, sledge, truck or barrow, with or without horses, or any beast of burden, to stand longer than is necessary for loading or unloading goods, or for taking up or setting down passengers (except hackney carriages and horses and other beasts of draught or burthen standing for hire in any place appointed for that purpose by lawful authority), and every person who by means of any cart, carriage, sledge, truck, or barrow, or any animal, or other means, wilfully interrupts any public crossing, or wilfully causes any obstruction in any public footpath, or other public thoroughfare . . .

Police are advised not to make unnecessary arrests:

The main object of an arrest is that the person should be made amenable to the law . . . Arrests should not be made for minor offences when the offender may be made amenable by summons. A constable has great powers of arrest, but he should exercise these powers with intelligence and discretion. (*Moriarty's Police Law*)

A classic example of the citizen who finally exhausts police patience is that of Gelberg v Miller 1961 1 WLR 153.

Mr Gelberg had parked in a restricted street while he enjoyed his lunch. Called out by police he said he would be leaving in three minutes but he needed to finish his coffee and to pay the bill. Threatened with the car's removal he coolly lifted the bonnet and removed the rotor arm. On emerging a second time he declined to provide his name and address. He was finally marched off under arrest—for obstructing police in the execution of their duty. The Lord

11

Chief Justice, Lord Parker, found the arrest justified but not for obstructing police, no breach of the peace having been threatened. The arrest was a proper one under the Metropolitan Police Act 1839:

> For anyone to leave his car in Jermyn Street at two o'clock in the afternoon in order that he may go in and have lunch in a nearby restaurant speaks for itself. It can and can only be a wilful obstruction of the highway.

Lord Parker commented 'whatever the true result of this case, if ever there was a case of a man in effect "asking for it", the appellant did.' (Mr Gelberg would of course today be able to use that statutory nuisance, the two-hour parking meter.)

Motorists are more likely to be arrested for non-payment of court fines than for misbehaviour in the street. Magistrates are constantly issuing bench warrants and these can be very embarrassing. Non-payment of a fixed penalty can lead to arrest if an offender goes on to ignore a summons and the subsequent court fine. There was even the case where an arrested defendant was entirely ignorant of the court proceedings as he had been also of the unpaid fixed penalty—and the notice to the owner, due to a change of address. The moral is always to notify both changes of ownership and changes of address—and to keep a record of the notification. (It is equally a precaution to keep a record of excess charges and of fixed penalty payments while it is always important when complying with an Owner Liability application to retain a copy of your answers to the various questions.)

Boarding and Alighting

The private motorist would find an Austin taxi an excellent investment. He would then find out what a lot he can get away with. Traffic wardens are always generous towards taxis, despite the fact that the law gives the taxi no special privileges. When it comes to picking up and setting down, the law is the same for all vehicles. The general rule is that

> Nothing shall render it unlawful to cause or permit a vehicle

to wait in any restricted street for so long as may be
necessary for the purpose of enabling any person to board
or alight from the vehicle or to load thereon or to unload
therefrom his personal luggage.

This was the London rule in 1960 and it remains to this day.
In some areas there is the added proviso that *no vehicle shall
wait for longer than two minutes,* 'or for such longer period
as a police constable in uniform or a traffic warden may
approve', while on clearways the maximum permitted stop
is two minutes dead.

The time for which a vehicle may wait was the subject
of the very first appeal taken by the AA to the High Court.
Mr Frederick Waterman has the honour of being the first
traffic warden whose duty came to be considered by Lord
Parker. It had happened on Saturday morning, 24 September
1960, at the end of the first week after war broke out in
the newly opened Mayfair meter zone.

Mr Clifford-Turner, bearer of a distinguished name among

solicitors, had driven to his flat to take his wife shopping. Traffic Warden Waterman had observed him alight and had duly timed the unattended vehicle. He could not be allowed to be loading or unloading, despite parcels and a pet dog, because the Commissioner had banned this activity, unless a goods vehicle was employed. Mr Clifford-Turner was a slow mover. He had only one lung and he had had to wait for the lift. It was all of five minutes before he emerged with his elderly wife. He declined to accept the £2 fixed penalty and he pleaded the picking up exception.

The magistrate made short work of the case. 'Persons to be picked up means persons who are ready and waiting to be picked up, not persons who might be ready in five, ten or twenty minutes'. The case was proved. There was an Absolute Discharge but on payment of 2 guineas costs. The whole of Mayfair was disgusted. It was 12 months before Lord Parker gave his ruling. The magistrate had been quite correct. It would be an 'impossible interpretation' to allow going up or down in a lift as part of boarding or alighting. The appeal was dismissed with expressions of sympathy for residents in meter zones. (Clifford-Turner v Waterman 1961 1 WLR 1499).

So passengers to be picked up must be waiting on the pavement. And their luggage? Must luggage be stacked ready to be picked up? The AA had another case on their hands when in 1962 Mr Tuke, a former chairman of Barclays Bank, had driven from his office in the City to collect by arrangement his personal luggage from the Connaught Hotel. While the luggage was being brought up from the baggage room Mr Tuke's attention was drawn to the fact that a traffic warden was fixing a penalty notice to his waiting Rolls. A period of six minutes was alleged. Mr Edward Robey, the Marlborough Street magistrate, dismissed the case. He thought the commonsense view was that, provided a motorist only waited for as long as was 'necessary' to load or unload luggage, he did not commit an offence, because that was a permitted exception to the general regulations. Tuke's case was a victory for commonsense.

As for the time allowed to 'alight', passengers in taxis are usually only too keen to get out quickly. But taxi drivers can have problems over finding the right change. There was the case in 1964 of the taxi driver who stopped on yellow lines to set down a fare who tendered a £5 note. The driver had to leave his cab while he sought change. He returned to find a police officer making out a four minute fixed penalty. The magistrate gave an Absolute Discharge but the driver appealed against the conviction, no doubt with help from the enterprising London Taxi Drivers' Aid Society. It seemed a certain winner but Lord Parker adopted the same hard line as in the appeal of Clifford-Turner. 'Alight' meant the purely physical act of getting out of the vehicle. The appeal was dismissed with a request that police might in future exercise more discretion. (Kaye v Hougham, a decision heavily criticised in 1964 CrLR 544).

Taxis may bask at parking meters, on payment, but cannot ply for hire. In many areas they are allowed to use bus lanes. Taxis are a form of public transport. It is no wonder that traffic wardens give taxi drivers the glad eye.

Breakdowns
No Waiting Orders do not all cater for the broken down vehicle. Law enforcement must however yield to common-sense. No magistrate would penalise a driver for something which was beyond his control. Many Orders do indeed specifically provide the following exception:

Nothing in this Order shall prevent any person from causing or permitting a vehicle to wait in any restricted street when the vehicle is waiting *owing to the driver being prevented from proceeding by circumstances beyond his control* or to such waiting being necessary in order to avoid an accident.

Traffic wardens do not normally question the precise reason for a breakdown. They do not enquire whether the situation might not have been avoided. But they are not gullible. 'Broken down. Gone for help' is a windscreen message which

15

may not be genuine. They will log the incident but if the vehicle is not gone within the hour they may issue a fixed penalty. The onus is then on the driver to prove his case. A breakdown service invoice is good enough to cancel any ticket but corroboration is normally essential in all cases.

Does running out of petrol constitute a breakdown? Motorway law certainly equates 'lack of fuel oil or water' with 'a breakdown or mechanical defect'. But ticket offices are not all sympathetic. In London the Central Ticket Office has taken the line that running out of petrol is avoidable. 'Running out of petrol is considered to be circumstances within the control of the driver and as such does not provide sufficient grounds upon which to recommence the withdrawal of the notice.' The point has yet to be tested in the High Court.

'Causing' Obstruction

When obstruction is caused by cars parked on both sides of the road, police don't usually stop to enquire who is responsible. They book the lot. This is one of the hazards of street parking, that you never know when some fool won't park on the other side.

But the law says you must not 'cause' your vehicle to

stand 'so as to cause' unnecessary obstruction. So it can be most unfair if you are punished for a situation of which you were not the cause. After all, in their own 'Misconception letter', do not police conclude with the very advice that can still lead to the motorist's downfall?

> It is a total misconception for any driver to suppose that parking is permitted whenever and wherever it is not specifically prohibited. Nothing could be further from the truth, for the basic principle always has been, and still remains, that the only place where a car may, with impunity, be left unattended on the carriageway, is in an authorised parking place and in accordance with the regulations governing that place. At all other times and places *it is the responsibility of a motorist leaving his car unattended, to ensure that by his action he does not cause obstruction.*

For years the AA had sought a ruling on this difficult question: the guilt of the motorist who was not the prime cause of an obstruction. It was in 1972 that an opportunity appeared to present itself. It was a Scottish case. Mr James Hardie, a resident in Musselburgh, had parked his car in a quiet street where, as the Case related 'residents regularly park their cars, to which the police have no objection so long as cars are not left directly opposite each other.' The magistrate had found as a fact that at about half past five when the car was parked there was no other car parked opposite. But two hours later a police patrol car could not get through. The driver of the opposite car 'pled' guilty and was fined £4. Mr Hardie was also prosecuted. He was found guilty and though granted an Absolute Discharge he appealed by Stated Case to the High Court of Justiciary. The Lord Justice Clerk 'withdrew' the magistrate's finding, taking the view that a resident who parks outside his own home could not be said thereby to cause unnecessary obstruction—an admirably commonsense view but one not likely to be followed south of the border.

In 1975 the AA had another shot. The Scottish case—Hardie v Leslie— had scored, but it went unreported. The

1975 appeal was to an English Crown Court, where scores do not have the prestige of a High Court decision but where a success can be cited. The facts of the case (Langham v Crisp 1975 CrLR 652) are so typical and the argument so lucid that they deserve quoting in full.

A motorist travelling along Kew Bridge Road and wishing to stop for lunch turned into Green Dragon Lane and parked in the first available space on the left-hand side. It was 12.30 p.m. There were no vehicles parked on the right-hand side of the road except for a car some 15 yards away. There were no cars parked in the vicinity.

Whilst the motorist was away having lunch another driver or drivers came and parked their cars opposite his, with the result that between 1.15 and 1.30 p.m. the road became congested and traffic was reduced to a single alternate line in either direction.

The motorist was prosecuted for causing his vehicle to stand on a road so as to cause unnecessary obstruction thereof, contrary to Regulation 114 of the Motor Vehicles (Construction and Use) Regulations 1973.

At the hearing before the justices evidence was given that Green Dragon Lane is just over 24 feet wide and is used mainly by residents of a nearby housing estate.

Each of the police witnesses conceded that he would not have prosecuted the defendant had there been only one line of parked cars between 1.15 and 1.30 p.m. The defendant was convicted and appealed.

It was contended on behalf of the appellant as follows: (1) that he "caused his vehicle to stand on a road" within the meaning of regulation 114 at the time when he first parked it; (2) that it could not be said at that point in time that his parking caused or was calculated to cause an unnecessary obstruction; and therefore (3) that he did not cause his vehicle to stand "so as to cause" an unnecessary obstruction within the meaning of the regulation. Alternatively, it was argued that if regulation 114 created a continuing offence, then it was wrong as a matter of principle to hold the appellant responsible for the acts of other drivers over whom he had no control, this being a necessary implication from a finding of guilt in the present circumstances.

Held, allowing the appeal, that at the time when Mr.

Langham parked his vehicle, he did not do so 'so as to cause' an unnecessary obstruction, and that was enough to dispose of the appeal.

Langham v Crisp scored a palpable hit. Prosecutors may have cause to groan but innocent motorists have cause to rejoice. Justice was done and seen to be done.

Costs

Every civilised ticket system permits an appeal to the courts. Some systems have a summons built into the ticket. Failure to pay at once sets the prosecution machinery into motion. The time, date and place of the court hearing is stated on the ticket. The minimum court fine is stated, often escalating according to the action taken by the accused. Attention is particularly drawn to the *costs* which may be added to the final penalty.

Our system is not like that at all. It only corresponds to the extent that the ticket holder is warned that in the event of non-payment 'the police may take proceedings'. There is no mention of the possible court fine nor of the liability to pay costs. It is over the *costs* element that any person minded to risk prosecution should be warned.

It is only recently that police prosecutors have begun to ask magistrates to award 'administration costs'. Some magistrates ask for a better explanation but many allow costs as a matter of course. The order is discretionary but if exercised properly there can be no appeal. The only law on the subject is that the order must be 'just and reasonable'. Costs must not be awarded as a penalty.

The AA made a stick for its own back when in 1960 it challenged a London stipendiary to explain an order for 2 guineas costs tacked onto a 20 shilling fine. It had seemed to the solicitor defending a traffic light summons that the costs had been awarded for wasting the court's time. No out of pocket expense had been claimed. So why the order? 'Because I say so', was the bleak reply. 'That is my order'. But all was explained in the affidavit sworn by the magistrate in the High Court proceedings to quash the order. Those drumming fingers were not a sign of impatience: they were simply calculating the cost to the Commissioner of making available the police constable. Two guineas was about right for his services. Despite some misgiving and with the aid of counsel as friend of the court, the order was upheld. It was judged not to be a disguised penalty (R v Burt *ex parte* Presburg. 1960 2 WLR 398).

If of course it can be believed that in police time it can cost up to £15 to enforce a penalty ticket, an order to pay £5 costs sounds not unreasonable. Whether it is just is another matter. If you go quietly you ought not to be penalised because others are obstreperous. If costs to the prosecutor are automatic, then by the same token the parking offender who beats the ticket should be similarly compensated. And as for an order to pay costs following an Absolute Discharge, this is the cause of much embittered feeling. It takes the gilt off the gingerbread.

The whole business of costs is getting out of hand. We should have Sutherland's Law. In Scotland the procurator fiscal gets no costs. He is a servant of the public, not of the police. Costs should be met from central funds.

Diplomats
Diplomats posted to London have a special parking problem. Their duties prevent travel on foot and their status prevents travel by public transport. Diplomats are constantly going the rounds, calling on each other and at Government Offices. Their transport must at all times be readily available. They get no concessions beyond the marked-out places reserved for the Ambassador or High Commissioner. Their misfortune is only relieved by the application of Diplomatic Immunity, the balm which avoids payment of parking fines.

The trouble is that there are too many people entitled to Diplomatic Immunity, and some are not too scrupulous about using the consular car on private occasions.

Diplomatic Immunity attaches to the person, not to the vehicle. CD plates are of no legal significance. The London

Diplomatic List, published by Her Majesty's Stationery Office and available to the public for 50p, contains an alphabetical list of the representatives of Foreign States and Commonwealth Countries in London 'with the names and designations of the persons returned as composing the establishment of their respective offices'. The list runs to a hundred pages, with the names, addresses and telephone numbers of the personnel in each of the 120-odd embassies, high commissions and international organizations. This includes the names of consorts (and of any imported, marriageable daughters). All, along with their cooks and bottlewashers, enjoy Diplomatic Immunity. They share the privilege expressed in the maxim of the learned Grotius in 1625:

The security of ambassadors is of more importance than the punishment of a particular crime.

21

This ancient tradition of immunity from a country's criminal jurisdiction is now well established. It cannot be waived, save by the foreign power. Representations may be made but diplomats do not normally appear in our criminal courts. (Their feet may not touch the ground before they get a home posting, though hardly for a parking violation.) All the same, the general view at the Court of St James is that parking fines ought to be paid. It is not playing the game to trump a fixed penalty by pleading Diplomatic Immunity. The doyen feels it is letting down the side. He has had occasion more than once to remind Corps members of Article 41 of the Vienna Convention on Diplomatic Relations, signed in 1961:

> It is the duty of all persons enjoying diplomatic immunity to respect the laws and regulations of the countries in which they are serving.

The parade of Misuse of Diplomatic Immunity takes place each year in the House of Commons. The Commissioner supplies the list of competitors, entrants from every country represented in London. The Home Secretary defers to diplomacy by listing the names in strict alphabetical order from Afghanistan to Zambia, with international organizations in the rear.

One of the earliest contests was in 1969 when Hungary was the winner with 2,601 unpaid penalties, Saudi Arabia second (1,729) and Poland (1,174) third. The USSR scored 130, the USA 57. In 1970 it was the turn of Ghana to win the crown; Hungary had to be content with second place and Nigeria was third. By 1973 the total number of fixed penalties cancelled had risen to over 48,000 and there was emerging a clear winner who was destined to retain the crown for every successive year: Miss Federal Republic of Nigeria (3,201), streets ahead of Cuba (2,163) and Cyprus (2,069). The USA scored only 65 to Soviet Russia's 421.

By this time international organizations were beginning to jump on the diplomatic bandwagon in earnest, useful scores being returned by the Commonwealth Secretariat and the International Coffee Organization. But Nigeria was the loss leader. In October and November 1975, when the fixed penalty had risen to £6, the loss to the British Treasury was over £60,000, for 10 per cent of which Nigerian diplomats were responsible (Hansard 29 Jan 1976). The anticipated loss for 1976, at the current going rate of 250 tickets daily, is £432,000.

This is not a problem peculiar to London. Washington has the same difficulty with foreign diplomats, but they are said to be solving it over there by removing enforcement from the criminal law. We could well follow suit.

Discs v Meters
We were all 'conned' into accepting the parking meter. The belief was that they were only temporary, designed to finance, and to subsidise, off-street parking. High rise multi-storey car parks, underground car parks, all would be available from the enormous revenue. But the first report from London gave a net profit of only £148,000 from a gross income of over half a million pounds, and even this was then subject to income and profits tax. It went from bad to worse, with 3 out of 10 London boroughs losing money and after 5 years from a revenue of over £3 million, less than £400,000 had gone towards off-street car parks. Then in 1967 came the Transport Bill, the proposal that parking meter revenue should be used for any transport purpose, condemned by the AA as 'a complete betrayal of all the undertakings ever given to the public and to Parliament'.

It is little wonder that in 1968 the City of Oxford preferred the parking disc to the parking meter. Of course the old Oxford v Cambridge rivalry had something to do with it. Cambridge had sold itself to the parking meter in 1964. Oxford sent delegates to Cheltenham and to Harrogate and they returned satisfied that a disc-controlled parking zone suited Oxford's image.

Cheltenham had been the pioneers of the disc, the system under which you set the time of your arrival on the rotating dial of a square of double thickness cardboard and this automatically shows the time of departure in the opposite window.

It is of French origin, *le disque de controle de stationnement.*
The advantages are quite simply that it is free, that is does not
require the unsightly and expensive parking meter and it offers
40 per cent more parking space. The argument against is that
meters give more precise control, yield revenue in an elastic
pricing policy and need only a third of the enforcement staff
required for disc control.

There are six specific disc offences:

Parking for longer than permitted;
Parking before the expiration of one hour after the vehicle
had been taken away;
Not displaying a parking disc;
Displaying a parking disc the times on which were not clearly
visible or did not indicate the half hour period during which the
vehicle arrived there;

The vehicle being of a class or description not authorised to be left there;
Parking in an incorrect position.

Enforcement is rigid at Oxford, where there are many painful 'slipped disc' cases. These may be less frequent when the British Standard No 4631 of 1970 is in more general use. The new disc shows the time of arrival only, a 12-hour disc divided into 15 minute sections, a *must* for commercial travellers for it is designed for national usage. It does however inhibit local advertising matter, a useful spin-off. Disc parking has now escaped its spa image. It is to be found also at Devizes, at Birkenhead and in Ripon.

History has not disclosed the inventor of the disc, but we know who is responsible for the meter. He is an American named Magee, and the first ever parking meter was installed in the City of Oklahoma in 1936. When County Hall decides finally to uproot the last of the London meters they are going to erect a statue to Magee. It should be tarred and feathered.

Doctors, the Disabled and Residents

There is an unwritten law for doctors, unwritten because doctors are difficult to pin down. The general instruction to traffic wardens is to give doctors' cars a wide berth. They know the doctor may be swinging the stethoscope but they give him the benefit of the doubt. They look for the BMA badge: Doctor visiting. This car will be moved as soon as possible.' 'Doctor on call.' These are the windscreen messages which do the trick. Are non-members of the BMA covered? Are radiologists, physiotherapists and ancillary workers covered? What about health visitors, midwives and nurses? All deserve concessions but they need to argue an urgent case to get a ticket cancelled.

Only, it seems, in Edinburgh, the cradle of the profession, is there a written law. The magnificent Corporation of Edinburgh Order, 1973, provides an exemption from waiting restrictions

when the vehicle is being driven by a medical practitioner visiting patients on professional calls in premises situated on any restricted road and the vehicle bears a badge approved by the Corporation conspicuously displayed on the nearside of the inside surface of the windscreen of the vehicle.

Dr Finlay would explode in Tannochbrae if a traffic warden dared to touch his car, but he gets no exemption when he visits Edinburgh.

In London the Harley Street consultant must use the Harley Garage. The GP who needs a car at his surgery must prove more than personal convenience to obtain, at a price, a marked out Doctor's Bay—available for 24 hours throughout the week, a concession many residents would willingly pay for.

The disabled are catered for by the national Orange Badge scheme which permits waiting for two hours on a yellow line, except where there is a ban on loading or unloading or in a bus lane. An orange disc similar to the one used in disc controlled areas is available.

Residents in meter zones have been a constant problem. It was not funny for late risers to have to dash out in pyjamas to move their cars. Private meters seemed a solution but meters would still require payment by 8.30 am, while there was also the resident working at home or whose wife used the car and wanted facilities to come and go at all hours. It was not until January 1968 that in London a residents' parking scheme was operated—the RESPARK scheme of cards and tokens, a constant headache for all concerned. Trespassers are prosecuted but residents' parking places remain a free-for-all outside controlled hours.

Residents must be grateful for small mercies. The GLC policy seems to be to chop down meters in residential areas. Life for the resident with no garage is no bowl of cherries.

Exceptions and Exemptions

The traffic warden who goes by the book is not popular. He is not popular with motorists and he can become very unpopular with his superiors. There was the authenticated case of Cyril the Zealot, the Dawlish traffic warden who was given the choice of resigning or moving ten miles away, to Newton Abbot. It was a difficult decision for the divisional police commander, for Cyril had done nothing wrong. There had just been too many complaints ·about his overzealous attentions to illegally parked vehicles. During his four years at Dawlish he had booked doctors, delivery men—and even a police car. This must have been the last straw.

Police have a great sense of humour. In 1975 the *Police Review* carried an excellent series of camera shots of a traffic warden ticketing a marked police car, with the caption 'How to make friends . . .' and a prize offered for the best comment from the driver. (Editorial discretion decided not to pursue the competition.) Police are well aware that they are not above the law. The exemption common to all No Waiting Orders is for 'vehicles when used for fire brigade, ambulance or police purposes' or as Edinburgh more precisely puts it 'vehicles *while being used*' for such purposes. A CID officer engaged on enquiries recently got costs against the police when prosecuted at Oxford for waiting in a restricted street. The exemption is available for the *authorised* use of a police officer's private car (Webb v Furber 1970 CrLR 283). On the other hand the young constable who claimed to have given himself permission to park was rightly convicted.

Of course the law would be an ass if it did not recognize certain exceptions from waiting restrictions, stopping to allow a person to board or alight or to load or unload personal luggage, stopping to avoid an accident, stopping to open a gate, exceptions for public service vehicles, post office vans, funeral cars. (When the police towed away the hearse, leaving the undertaker holding the coffin, the magistrate voiced the general indignation that the police should prosecute. 'It is a shame this case ever came to court.') But the private motorist, however essential to him is the use of his car, gets no exemption—unless he can argue that his use can be equated with that of the police or the ambulance service. The private car is forever being used in emergencies—but the law recognizes no emergencies. (The air correspondent of the BBC was rightly angry when the Central Ticket Office refused to cancel a ticket for a call on a chemist to collect emergency medicine.)

It is the business user who considers himself most hardly hit by the law of the yellow line. When the special problems of the commercial traveller were debated the Ministry spokesman felt obliged to point out that in the community there are many groups of people with special problems:

> . . . for instance, window cleaners, people putting up advertising posters, funeral directors, chimney sweeps, television and radio repairmen, plumbers, knife grinders, veterinary surgeons, masseurs who make visits for an hour or half an hour each, and even journeymen gardeners who call for short periods of time. All these people, in our crowded city streets, would consider they have some right of priority—as well as doctors and district nurses.

He went on:

> It does not really matter who is in the car or who owns the

car; the problem is that a car is a piece of machinery, and on the roadside in a busy centre causes obstruction. I have every sympathy with these people. I should like to give many, many people exemptions, but I fear that it is one of the penalties of our modern urban life that people have to change their ways in carrying out their business.

But fortunately this is not quite the last word. All No Waiting Orders carry the exemption that *nothing in the order shall apply to anything done with the permission or at the direction of a police officer in uniform or of a traffic warden.* In the absence of police or traffic wardens a polite windscreen message can often work wonders.

Excise Licence Display

'Pay and Display' is as much the rule for the excise licence as it is in those car parks which make it an offence not to display the adhesive ticket.

The offence punished by the traffic warden is stated on the fixed penalty notice: 'The vehicle was on a road without an Excise Licence being exhibited on it in the prescribed manner, contrary to s. 12(4) of the Vehicles (Excise) Act 1971'. And it is usual to add 'This matter will be reported to the Motor Licensing Dept.'

What is the prescribed manner? The law says that the licence shall be fixed to the vehicle in a holder sufficient to protect the licence from any effects of the weather to which it would otherwise be exposed and shall be exhibited in the case of any vehicle fitted with a glass windscreen *on or adjacent to the nearside lower corner of the windscreen, so that all particulars thereon are clearly visible by daylight from the nearside of the road.*

As Lord Widgery was later to point out, 'failure to exhibit' is not a crime in the ordinary sense. He called it 'quasi-criminal', belonging to that class of offence for which there is absolute liability but which involved no 'moral stigma'. This is small comfort to the person who, perhaps innocently, has no licence, or no current licence, to exhibit, or to the unlucky person who has displayed the licence but due to

no human intervention it has slipped in its plastic holder to the floor of the vehicle. (Strowger v John 1974 RTR 124). However, the fact remains that at present there is just no defence to 'failure to exhibit', save only when the licence is necessarily removed for renewal at a post office or when the vehicle is taken for a compulsory test. Even when the fourteen days grace period is given statutory effect the old licence will still need to be displayed and there will need to be proof that application has been made. 'Licence applied for' is of dubious value.

Lord Widgery has also had to explain that not only is 'failure to exhibit' an offence of absolute liability though not strictly 'criminal' but the revenue penalty which may follow is not a fine 'in the conventional sense'. (Pilgram v Dean 1974 2 AER 751). The significance of this is that you cannot complain if you are made to suffer twice for what appears to be one offence. The offences are not in the alternative but are cumulative. It is all very hard.

It is of course the revenue offence that is the serious 'crime', for which the law provides a penalty of £50, or a fine up to five times the duty chargeable plus any back duty, though for a mere oversight with no loss of revenue the taxation authority may offer a mitigated penalty.

It was on account of the notorious avoidance of car tax that it was decided in 1970 to include the hitherto rarely prosecuted offence of simple 'failure to exhibit' among the functions of the traffic warden and make it punishable by the fixed penalty. It was the first departure from what was never a normal police function, that of tax collection. But local authorities even with bands of civilian detectives had been unable to cope. The news that traffic wardens could issue tickets spread like wildfire, and as with the arrival of the television detector van it led to a salutary stampede to renew or take out the car licence. By 1973 over 400,000 cases in the London area alone came under investigation.

Even the best people can be forgetful. There was the report of the motorist who angrily left the court and ventured onto the magistrates' car park. He was delighted to find the Chairman's car with a licence six weeks out of date. He took much pleasure in reporting the quasi-criminal to the proper authority!

Fines On-The-Spot
No one enjoys getting a 'ticket' but all agree that a ticket system makes sense. It avoids all the cumbersome procedure of a prosecution. It acts like a tonic. It is a mild dose and when taken in the right spirit it purges the system. Enthusiasts consider it could well be extended to other offences, such as dropping litter or allowing the dog to foul the pavement.

Of course pure-minded lawyers are not so enthusiastic. Any system which tends to short circuit justice can be dangerous. As with any short circuit there is the risk of fire. Our ticket system is surrounded by safety devices, but it is still a police procedure. Compared with some ticket systems it is a pearl of a procedure, though traffic wardens might consider that it is cast before too many unappreciative swine, because recipients just fail to realise that our system is not a 'fine-on-the-spot'. It is a Fixed Penalty Notice, a fine distinction.

The Fixed Penalty Notice has its roots in ancient law.

It goes back to 1825, if not earlier, when Commissioners of Customs and Excise were permitted to 'stay sist or compound' proceedings out of court. The opportunity was given to avoid prosecution on payment of a penalty. This compromise was suggested by Sir Reginald Sharpe QC and his committee in 1955. It was considered that what was good enough for smugglers should be good enough for motorists. It is a power exercised to this day by local tax offices, pursuant to s.3(2) of the Vehicles Excise Act 1971. The letter to the tax offender reads:

> Having regard to the circumstances the council have decided to offer you the opportunity of paying a mitigated penalty. You are not bound to accept this offer, but if you wish the matter to be disposed of in this way, payment should be made within fourteen days. If payment is not made by that date, it will be assumed that you do not wish to avail yourself of this offer and legal proceedings will be taken against you.

This is precisely similar to the offer made by the traffic warden in his Fixed Penalty Notice, a Notice not of a violation as on the crude fine-on-the-spot but a Notice of Opportunity, a highly civilised procedure.

Still, call a ticket by any other name—it smells the same. It *is* a penalty, on the spot. It demands money, with menaces. It is no more than a system of very rough justice.

Footpaths and Verges

It is splendid news that at long last it may become legal to park on a footway or verge. Local authorities are empowered under provisions in the Road Traffic Act 1974 to make orders exempting streets at all times or during specified periods from the new law which, when it comes into force, will prohibit vehicles generally from parking on verges, central reservations and footways unless loading or unloading when this could not have been carried out satisfactorily elsewhere, provided the vehicle is not left unattended, on pain of a summary fine of £100.

No motorist ever really supposed it could be legal to park on the footway. It just seems so very often the sensible thing to do. Unfortunately many police forces do not see it in this light. Some have quite a 'thing' about footpath parking, be the encroachment ever so minimal. One wheel is enough to bring down a charge of obstruction. It could be an offence under section 78 of the Highway Act 1835 or section 28 of the Town Police Clauses Act 1847, with the Metropolitan Police Paving Act, 1817, section 65, held in reserve. But the more common prosecution is for causing unnecessary obstruction under the Construction and Use Regulations, for it has been solemnly held that 'road' includes the footway as well as the carriageway (Bryant v Marx 1932 AER 518).

Normally a police caution is sufficient to stop the practice. There is however the remarkable case of Worth v Brooks (1959 CrLR 885) where a certain Mr Worth told the police just what they could do with a caution for parking on a grass verge.

It all arose from an occasion in December 1958 when Mr Worth, along with other brethren, had parked his car on the grass verge while attending a masonic meeting. We are not told his office in the Lodge. We only know that the meeting was rudely interrupted. On enquiry from the Worshipful

Master as to who it was who sought admission he was told it was the police. Solomon's Temple was overturned in the rush for the door, the brethren calling loudly on the Great Architect. But Brother Worth stood his ground. He admitted the car had been there for five hours but he could not see any obstruction. He would not accept a Caution. He was duly summoned, pleaded Not Guilty and was granted an Absolute Discharge. It was not that the AA was a hotbed of free-masonry, even if their telegraphic address was Fanum ('temple'), but they saw the case as deserving their support. They briefed a future Solicitor General, Sir Arthur Irvine QC, but Lord Parker turned down his thumb. Worth v Brooks appears in all the textbooks, supporting the proposition that the grass verge is part of the highway. (Contrary to general belief the appellant was unrelated to Mr Harry Worth, the TV comedian.)

Pedestrianisation is all the vogue today—the creation of precincts and the orders made under powers in the Town and Country Planning Act 1968 to extinguish vehicle rights over highways. So it seems only fair to allow the motorist something in return. The new law promises a foot in the door to better things. It is at least one tyre on the kerb.

Foreign Visitors

A few select traffic wardens (the glamorous ones working in London's West End) are entrusted with the Commissioner's Greeting, a model of diplomacy—his Police Notice composed in four languages, English, French, German and Italian:

> The Commissioner of Police of the Metropolis welcomes you to London and hopes that you are enjoying your visit. He would like to warn you, however, that by leaving your car here you are liable to prosecution for a parking offence. No action will be taken this time, but the Commissioner hopes that you will be careful to observe the traffic laws in future.

'The following information', adds the Commissioner, 'may be helpful':

In most areas of central London parking is controlled by parking meters. Between 08.30 and 18.30 hours cars can be parked only at a meter; for which a small charge is made. After 18.30 it is advisable still to leave your car at a meter; there is no charge in the evening.

The Notice concludes with a warning:

If your car is left so as to cause serious obstruction, it may be removed by the police. Enquiry of a police officer or at the nearest police station will tell you where it is and you will be liable to pay a removal charge when you collect it.

This warning that the car may be removed is not an idle threat. 'Serious obstruction' is not the only ground for removal. Any infringement will do. By hook or by crook the removal squad will break and enter. One minute to master the controls and it's away to the police pound. Fifteen pounds is the price to pay—*frais de déplacement—Rückforderung Abschleppgebühren—Le sara indicato dove potra ricuperare.* No foreign currency is refused.

But short of towing away the foreign visitor's car there is no redress. It is really not fair; their immunity is not reciprocal. Many a British motorist has had to turn out his pockets to a foreign traffic warden. But parking offenders in Britain must be given the statutory 21 days to pay a fixed penalty, and by the time the enforcement machinery grinds into action the foreign visitor has escaped our jurisdiction.

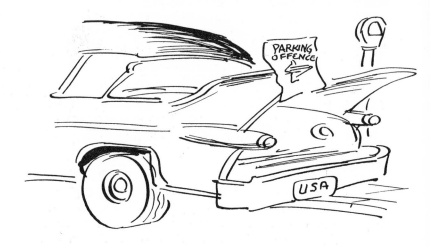

A parking offence is not extraditable. EEC regulations may yet alter that one. Meantime the wardens who are not issued with the Commissioner's Greeting must stick £6 tickets on foreign cars. You never know, there may be some honest soul who will have the decency to pay up.

Know Your Traffic Signs
Parking law is riddled with signs and roadmarkings. There are for example at least six basic types of local restrictions, each with its own arrangement. There are two-tier restrictions on waiting, signed by yellow lines and time plates. There are three-tier restrictions on loading, marked by blips on the kerb. There are no-stopping clearways, marked by signs without yellow lines. There are peak hour clearways *with* yellow lines. There are also bus clearways. And there can be temporary restrictions signed by police 'No Waiting' cones.

In addition there are a further five instances where rules and signs not imposed specifically to prohibit waiting do nevertheless have this effect. These are on motorways, at zebra crossings, at pelican crossings, in bus lanes and opposite double white lines.

On clearways the rule varies according to whether it is in an urban area or in the country. Urban clearways are commonly found in large towns on radial routes. They allow no stopping at peak hours on the carriageway or verges except for up to two minutes to pick up or set down passengers. Clearways in rural areas are marked by the 'no stopping' sign (a diagonal red cross on blue, circled in red) repeated at intervals. They mean no stopping on the carriageway, except in a lay-by—not even to set down a passenger. Bus stop clearways are marked by a broad yellow line and time plate—no stopping allowed from 7 am to 7 pm.

Motorway rules prohibit stopping except in an emergency on the hard shoulder or verge. Drowsy drivers must *not* park (Higgins v Bernard 1972 RTR 304). No signs are provided apart from those indicating the commencement of motorway regulations, the international motorway symbol.

Zebra pedestrian crossing regulations prohibit waiting, setting down or picking up either passengers or goods within the zig-zag marked area on both the approach and exit sides of the crossing.

At pelican pedestrian crossings no waiting is permitted between the approach studs and the crossing.

Central double white lines used to separate opposing traffic flows where visibility is restricted prohibit waiting, even when the broken line is on the driver's side, except to pick up or set down passengers or goods, if there is no convenient lay-by.

It is obviously essential to know your traffic signs and this is indeed the title to the supplement to the *Traffic Signs Regulations and General Directions 1975* which runs to 200 pages and costs £3.50. *Know Your Traffic Signs* costs only 40p, fully illustrated. It is produced by the Department of the Environment and is so lively that it cannot be long before the Department produces a boardgame, the No Waiting game.

The No Waiting game would be played on a board, similar to Monopoly, laid out with traffic signs. The players would represent police, traffic wardens and motorists. The object of the game would be to circle the board without incurring a penalty. The player would need to provide the correct answer to every problem posed by the traffic sign. If correct he can decide whether to stay put and take a chance or have another throw. It could be very educational. Players would not be sent to jail but there would be towaway zones, car pounds and parking meters. It could be played with real money. No cheating would be allowed but each player could decide when to play his Joker, Diplomatic Immunity by motorists, Causing Obstruction by police.

Sadly, such a game is not yet a commercial proposition. We have yet to decide our attitude to the Geneva Protocol on Road Markings. Until all signs are standardized the No Waiting game is not for export. We shall have to wait a few years for *Jeux sans frontières*!

Loading and Unloading
Scotland Yard was not bluffing when in 1973 they warned that in future traffic wardens in Central London would *shoot on sight*. The traditional delay of 10 or 20 minutes would no longer be allowed. They explained the reasons for this in a press release:

> This move is designed to separate the illegal parkers from genuine cases of loading and unloading. There is a widespread impression among motorists that cars may wait on yellow lines provided that they do not stay for more than 20 minutes. Some drivers believe that they are allowed 10 minutes grace. Both impressions are wrong.

In the past traffic wardens have usually given 10 minutes constant or 20 minutes casual observation, to vehicles which they suspect of illegal parking, in order to establish whether or not loading or unloading is taking place before issuing a ticket. This practice may have helped to create motorists' misconceptions. In fact vehicles may wait in many places where there are yellow lines but only if loading or unloading is really necessary, with a limit of 20 minutes after 11 am. In Soho private cars may not wait even for this purpose: the concession is limited to goods vehicles. In certain places, which are marked by signs, loading and unloading from any type of vehicle is prohibited.

This practice by wardens will not be new: for about two years they have been issuing tickets on sight but this has so far been confined to areas of special difficulty. Senior police officers have however been increasingly concerned about the accident hazard and obstruction that arises from vehicles parked illegally for comparatively short periods. It has therefore been decided that the law in this respect must be enforced more rigorously throughout the Metropolitan Police District.

The press release said that if a driver who was 'genuinely' engaged in loading or unloading received a ticket he should write to the Central Ticket Office 'giving the facts and mentioning any evidence that would support what he says'.

Now it is not supposed that these London tactics are employed generally, and it is likely that in more civilised areas traffic wardens do continue to 'log first' and 'shoot later'. However, it has to be conceded that Scotland Yard has a point. The law is clear enough: it is for the motorist to prove an exemption, not for the traffic warden to exclude its possibility. (Funnell v Johnson 1962 CrLR 488). The three-minute ticket, or indeed a one-minute ticket is perfectly 'legal'. But is it playing the game?

Play in Leicester was conducted more fairly. These were the written instructions issued to traffic wardens:

Loading and unloading—The Order does not attempt to define loading or unloading. You will ordinarily not find it necessary at all to enquire about vehicles obviously built for the carriage of goods, e.g., lorries, vans and so on, unless you have reason to believe that they are not actually being loaded or unloaded. When deciding whether private cars can reasonably be said to be loading or unloading, ask yourself if the car appears to be necessary—as distinct from convenient—for that purpose. In a large and wealthy city like Leicester, large sums of money are frequently deposited at banking houses by car or collected from them by the same means; it is obviously better for security and for crime prevention if motor transport can be used for this purpose. It is therefore the practice generally to extend the discretion vested in police in respect of loading or unloading to vehicles left outside banking houses for not more than 20 minutes for this purpose.

This makes sense, especially the bit about *necessary* as distinct from *convenient*. It accords with Sprake v Tester (1959 CrLR 509) where it was held that a parcel of 6 champagne glasses did not come within the exemption. It could have been carried. 'But', said Lord Goddard, 'I can understand a private car coming along with a load of things inside—it might be a piece or two of furniture—it might be half a dozen pictures to be reframed or cleaned. I would not even exclude a heavy laundry basket. There may be many cases in which the motor car would be used for something which it would not be reasonable for anybody to carry in his hand.'

As for using the car to collect large sums of money there is now a High Court ruling. By a majority decision it has been decided that the exemption from waiting restrictions does *not* apply in such a case. It is *the vehicle* as distinct from *the driver* which is covered. Notes and coin can be carried on the person. A car is not necessary (Richards v McKnight 1976 CrLR 749).

The fact is that essential use of a private car for loading and unloading or collecting and delivering is never easy to justify. You can delay action by a windscreen message or the open boot but if you're not back to the car very swiftly you can well find you've been shot down.

Permission to wait for any transaction can be granted. The problem is to find a p.c. or a warden when he's wanted. They're usually around only when they are *not* wanted!

40

Magistrates

Police and traffic wardens may act with humanity. Magistrates, on the other hand, act like robots. They have no feelings, only rubber stamps. There are exceptions but generally this is the rule, that police and traffic wardens can exercise discretion but that it is more than a magistrate's job is worth to temper justice with mercy. It is the fault of the ticket system and it was foreseen long ago. It was in 1962 that a metropolitan chief clerk wrote in the Criminal Law Review:

Either it (the magistrates court) must act, in effect, as a rubber stamp endorsing, with a suitable deterrent addition, the mechanical operation of the system; or it must bring about the collapse of the system which is ultimately bound to ensue if offenders discover they have a very good chance of being fined less than the fixed penalty provided they let the law take its lengthy and laborious course.

He concluded:

Whichever choice the court makes, it risks bringing the administration of justice into confusion and disrepute. It seems very doubtful whether a fixed penalty system can ever be successfully linked with the normal discretionary penalty procedure of our criminal courts.

It was not until 1970 that the law permitted the prosecution to mention the issue of a 'ticket'. For ten years magistrates were expected to be ignorant of the lost opportunity to settle out of court. They were supposed to deal with cases *on their merits*. It was expected to be a Bad Day at Bow Street when the Chief Magistrate lent his prestige to the trial of the first ticket test cases in November 1960. He would show how to deal with holders of £2 fixed penalties who exercised their right to be prosecuted. The first case concerned the delivery of a case of kippers to a Mayfair restaurant. Had the driver employed a 2-ton truck he would have been within his rights, but he had used his private car. He was fined £3 and costs. Similar penalties followed but police smiles wore off when one defendant was fined no more than the fixed penalty while there were black looks over the first Absolute Discharge. London stipendiaries followed the lead. They refused to be cowed by the fixed penalty. Penalties reflected the circumstances of the offence and of the offender. Justice was seen to be done.

Times have now changed. Magistrates are browbeaten by lectures to cane motoring offenders more heavily. They are obsessed with the notion of standard penalties. The Magistrates Association reminds members of the maximum fine for every offence, makes suggestions for starting prices and encourages a local 'tariff'. There might as well be fixed penalties for every offence. And it is not cheaper to plead guilty. It is cheaper to pay up while there is the opportunity.

Magistrates take their job very seriously. They lean over backwards to be fair to both sides. If they dismiss very few cases it is because very few parking cases permit any real defence. It is rarely oath against oath. There has been only one recorded case where a magistrate was so unwise as to express aloud what others may think but prefer to keep to themselves, and the case did not concern a traffic warden.

> Quite the most unpleasant cases we have to decide are those where the evidence is a direct conflict between a police officer and a member of the public. My principle in such cases has always been to believe the evidence of the police officer, and therefore we find the case proved.

This, said the Divisional Court, 'clearly amounted to bias' and the conviction was quashed. (R v Bingham Justices 1974, *The Times* 3 July).

There are some 20,000 magistrates in England and Wales, 13,000 men to 6,500 women, sitting part time and unpaid in 680 Divisions, some sitting daily, some weekly, some fortnightly. They usually sit three on a bench, to avoid a split decision. Two thirds of their work is taken up with motoring offences, much of it very minor. The work is 'monotonous mechanical and excruciatingly boring', so it was said by a JP in a recent letter to *The Times*.

The statistics of parking cases for 1975 dealt with by

42

magistrates do rather bear this out. They are as follows:

Prosecutions	Offences	Findings of guilt
32,116	Meter zone offences	30,612
1,478	Dangerous position	1,304
31,248	Obstruction	30,352
128	Heavy commercials on verges or footways	124
19,129	Failure to park on the nearside after dark	18,780
1,011	Stopping on clearways	970
81,023	Offences against waiting restrictions	76,842

A hundred and fifty thousand cases uses up an awful lot of rubber stamps, which is just about the extent of the magistrates' work when 90 per cent of offenders plead guilty. How some 7,000 managed to escape is the only mystery.

In London much of the work is handled by 39 metropolitan stipendiaries (only two women) who sit alone and who are, after all, paid to be bored. They too hand out rubber-stamp justice. Mitigating circumstances? Nothing can mitigate the offence of wasting the court's time when there was the opportunity to settle out of court.

Meter Maids
It is sheer cruelty to tie down traffic wardens to parking meters. They don't like it and they don't like being called 'meter maids'. In the United States and in Australia this may be appropriate but not in Britain. In Britain we have controlled parking zones where parking elsewhere than at a meter is an offence. It is what goes on away from meters that should be the traffic warden's main concern. She does not expect to be employed simply to milk excess charges. That is the local authority's job. She has only to look at her terms of reference to see this confirmed. She was created to help the police in the control and regulation of traffic. It is only as an afterthought that it is said that wardens *may* be employed as—

the worst indignity—'school crossing patrols' or lollipop ladies, while 'under arrangements made with the Minister or a local authority' they *may* be employed as parking attendants at street parking places.

Of course it should never have been allowed from the start. From 1958 for two years Westminster employed their own staff to supervise the meters. Then in 1960 the Commissioner took over that responsibility, and of course the meter takings dropped dramatically. A warden can't be in two places at

once and control of traffic takes priority. The Commissioner soon regretted it and from 1968 onwards he seems to have been trying to tell local authorities to wake up, threatening in effect that if they would not look after the meters he could not help them out in their plans for extensions. He put it like this in one of his Annual Reports:

> The chief advantage of a withdrawal of traffic wardens from meter attendants' duties would be that it would release traffic wardens for redeployment and enable wardens employed on enforcement of waiting restrictions to be deployed more selectively and thus over a wider area.

The meter attendant element of traffic wardens' duties involves the regular inspection of the meters and the vehicles parked at them and as long as wardens are tied to meter supervision, little flexibility of deployment is possible to enable waiting restrictions to be better enforced . . . It seems to me indefensible that scarce police resources should be employed on regulating the use of space within parking places and ensuring that Councils receive the money owing to them.

Quite evidently police prefer their traffic wardens to be free range. They are not interested in quantity—masses of municipal eggs in the shape of excess charges. The retort from local authorities is that battery birds cost police less—on account of the municipal contribution. You can't have it both ways.

'Meter Out of Order'

The law recognizes that the parking meter is no more than a piece of clockwork, requiring constant inspection and maintenance.

Before a parking meter is brought into use the parking authority shall make arrangements for testing by the insertion in the meter of a coin of the appropriate denomination and the timing of the performance of the mechanism contained in the meter by a reliable stopwatch or clock. . . . After a parking meter is brought into use, the parking authority shall make arrangements for ensuring
(a) the case of the meter is kept in a clean condition and that any instructions are easily legible
(b) the winding of the mechanism of the meter, if it is of the automatic type and is not electrically controlled, once in every seven days or more often if necessary
(c) the inspection at intervals of not more than four weeks of the meter to ascertain whether it is in proper working order, and
(d) the removal at intervals of not more than one year of the mechanism from the case of the parking meter.

But despite all this testing and maintenance the law accepts that meters can become out of order. Parking meters are not infallible, as a certain Judge Bloch found some years ago. The law says that if a meter is found to be out of order on any routine inspection *or on any other occasion* the parking authority is required to take steps to put it into proper working order 'and meantime to place over the meter a hood or other cover to prevent the insertion of a coin'. (A green canvas or plastic hood is often used. In the City of London they use a cunning green plug inserted into the coin orifice, gaily marked '2 hours free parking').

What should the meter-parker do if there is no official out of order notice but he can't insert the coin? The law says that the parking authority 'may at each meter provide a notice giving the name, address and telephone number of the person to be notified', a precaution which is generally neglected. So in default the accepted practice is simply to explain the difficulty in a windscreen message, e.g. meter jammed, preferably giving the time and date of parking. Some put 'Unable to insert coin. I am at such-and-such an address. Kindly tell me when meter is cleared'. Traffic wardens must exercise their own judgment. They are not usually instructed to test out the meter. They can tell the truth of the situation through the tell-tale peephole. 'Out of Order' messages are usually genuine. The meter will be bagged and the fault reported. When it will be repaired is another matter.

Meter Payment

The law requires parking authorities to provide on every meter a notice stating the hours of operation, the authorised charges and 'such information as to offences and other matters relating to the parking place as they think fit.' No one has ever complained that this tall order is not adequately fulfilled. The rules as to payment are set out briskly:

> Free use of unexpired time. Coin to be inserted at time of parking. Subsequent insertion of coin is an offence. At the end of free time or time paid for an excess charge is incurred.

In some areas, as in central London, a plate may be added: 'Pre-payment only. Meter feeding prohibited.' Few people make any mistake over the initial payment. Normally they are only too glad to find a vacant meter, hoping for unexpired time but ready to pay—if they have the correct coins. The defence of leaving the meter only to get change was exploded in 1961 (Strong v Dawtry 1961 1 AER 296). The law was applied strictly. The offence is 'leaving the vehicle, the initial charge not having been duly paid.' As Lord Parker CJ said:

> No element of reasonable time can be imported unless it be such reasonable time as is involved in getting out of the driving seat and putting the coin into the meter: in other words, between stopping the car and stepping on the pavement and inserting the coin.

Meter-feeding is quite another matter. By now, everyone should know that this is an offence. It is never done innocently, except perhaps at two-stage meters where you have not got the second coin. The law says however that 'where more than one coin is required for payment the coins should be so inserted in the parking meter *one immediately after the other.*' Nor may you return before unexpired time has run out and insert a coin. It must be pre-payment on leaving the vehicle.

The main meter manufacturers, Messrs Venners Limited, in their lively booklet entitled *The Metered Parking System* (probably now out of print, the market having rather dried up) had warned customers about meter-feeding in no uncertain terms:

> It should be stressed that great efforts should be made to detect offenders especially those people who make it a daily habit, since this offence strikes at the roots of meter parking schemes and if unchecked can bring a scheme into disrepute.

Meter-feeding is spelt out very clearly:

No person shall insert in the parking meter relating to

the bay in which the vehicle is left any coin additional to the coin or coins inserted by way of payment of the initial charge in respect of that vehicle.

It matters not that the meter-feeder never made any initial payment. He is deemed to have done so.

Of course it is a difficult offence to detect. Parking attendants patrol in plain clothes like store detectives. Plain clothes police keep observation. Traffic wardens issue excess charges. Cars are towed away, but it goes on. The meter-feeder or nickel-hog is a desperate character. Any person 'whether being the driver of a vehicle or not' may be prosecuted.

'Meter Suspended'
Powers to suspend meters are very wide. 'Any duly authorised person' may suspend the use of a parking meter 'when-

ever he considers such suspension reasonably necessary'. The possible reasons are listed in the Parking Order—facilitating the movement of traffic or promoting its safety, building operations, road maintenance, furniture removal—these are obvious. Less obvious are 'occasions on which it is likely by reason of some special attraction that any street will be thronged or obstructed', a regular occurrence at film premières in London's West End. (Shutting down all the meters from lunchtime in Leicester Square once led to Questions in the House). Private applications may be made for weddings or funerals or on other 'special occasions'. In Edinburgh a wedding is not treated as a funeral but it can still be a 'special occasion'.

The suspension is indicated by a hood 'or other cover', often by a red bag, padlocked. The penalty for debagging a meter is £20. Parking at a suspended meter usually leads to the car being towed away. It is a fixed penalty offence. But a suspended bay is still a 'parking place' and loading or unloading there is not an offence (Wilson v Arnott *The Times*, 2 November 1976).

Meter Vandals
It is an ill wind that does no good at all. Meters plugged with chewing gum, the mechanism jammed with matchsticks, beer can rings and other foreign objects, smashed meter dials, all render the meter Out of Order.

In the London borough of Islington the vandals are said not to be content with wanton damage. Gangs have been reported using skeleton keys and hammers. In 1971, after spending £5,000 in repairs over a period of only three months, the Islington council decided to pack it in and announced free parking for six months on half its sites. Their bright idea of selling discs to motorists was not approved by the GLC.

But Liverpool is said to be the worst hit by vandals. They would stop at nothing, certainly not when there were loaded meters for the taking. Boston (Mass) was consulted. There they have vandal-resistant meters, the coins encased in a heavy iron box. Boston vandals continue to uproot 200 meters a

year but if recovered the takings are always intact. Such meters are expensive, which may explain why Liverpool seems to be the only area which never makes a meter profit, apart of course from Islington.

What are the motorist's rights when the meter, post and all, has been stolen or is removed by the council for repair? It seems, and Lord Parker was not too certain, that unless the council marks the bay as 'suspended' parkers may park freely. (Roberts v Powell 1966 CrLR 225).

Meters: Hours of Operation

There is no universal rule governing hours of operation. Few meters operate earlier than 8 am and most close down at 6 or 6.30 pm. You need to watch it on Saturdays, when some finish for the afternoon but others work late. Sundays are usually free of charge, but not everywhere. At the seaside Sunday may be just the day for the meters to cash in, on the seafront at Brighton for example where until 1964 the meters ran for 365 days in the year until they were persuaded to take a rest on Christmas Day and Boxing Day.

In urban areas meters all proclaim 'No charge on Sundays

and Bank Holidays'. These are Red Letter Days for meter users. In England we have five statutory bank holidays: New Year's Day, Easter Monday, the Spring Holiday, the Late Summer Holiday and Boxing Day. Good Friday and Christmas Day are 'common law' holidays, hallowed by tradition. It is more complicated in Scotland, where the meters do not appear to recognize Boxing Day or Easter Monday, but in Edinburgh they have Victoria Day while there is also the Glasgow Fair Holiday. Also the Queen's Birthday. They are very canny in Scotland and many a Scot has moaned over the sixpence that went bang on crossing the border.

The meaning of 'bank holiday', meterwise, was settled in

O'Neill v George 1969 CrLR 202. There had been a gold crisis in March 1968 and in the small hours the Queen had signed a Royal Proclamation to enable banks to close in order to fix the price of gold. The action was taken under the Bank Holidays Act 1871. This led to a wild rumour that parking meters were free of charge. The Central Ticket Office prosecuted a solicitor for non-payment. The stipendiary magistrate found there was indeed an ambiguity and awarded 30 guineas costs to the defendant. Excess charges were frozen throughout the country until Lord Parker breathed life into them. The Bank Holiday Act dealt with finance and banking. Parking meter orders dealt with traffic. Appeal allowed but no order as to costs.

So now model Orders explain bank holidays as meaning 'public holidays'. This made sense until a Leeds solicitor tested the Tuesday following the Summer Bank Holiday, and won his case. The appeal, The Lord Mayor, Aldermen and Citizens of the City of Leeds v Victor David Zermansky, was finally abandoned. If a day is locally recognized as a public holiday, then the meters are free of charge.

Future royal jubilees are another example of extra bank holidays—national holidays. Traffic wardens will no doubt be lining the route but they may also be on parking duty, because it is not unlikely that the use of parking meters will be suspended during the celebrations.

Meters: 'Manner of Waiting'

Every meter Order carries a regulation entitled 'Manner of Waiting', which is really no more than to say in a hundred words that every part of the vehicle must be parked within the marked out bay. This is never an easy manoeuvre, particularly with bigger cars. Local authorities have become increasingly mean over the space provided. The original lengths of bays were all around 20 feet, but now many have been reduced to 16 feet. Meters do not seem properly to cater for Cadillacs. However chauffeurs are known to study Orders carefully and they will have noted that in many Orders it is stated that 'Every part of the vehicle must normally be within the limits of the parking bay—*unless its length precludes compliance*'. In such a case the vehicle should be parked so that 'the longitudinal axis of the vehicle is parallel to the edge of the carriageway nearest to the vehicle and the distance between the said edge and the nearest wheel of the vehicle is not more than 12 inches'. (A footrule is to be found in the pouch of every good meter maid). Chauffeurs will also note that 'where the metered parking bay is at right angles to the kerb the back of the vehicle must be nearest to the kerb *and not projecting over the footway*'.

The penalty for improper parking can be a court fine up to £20, or a fixed penalty and a tow-away.

Meters: The National League
Parking meters in Britain have sufficiently settled down for it to be possible to allocate them in Divisions, the heavy areas with more than a thousand meters in the First Division, those with five hundred to a thousand in the Second Division and those with less than five hundred in the Third Division. The figures are on a 1975 meter count.

First Division

Westminster - - - - -	10,726
Kensington and Chelsea -	5,400
Camden - - - - -	4,181
Birmingham City - - -	3,742
Manchester United - - -	2,500
Leeds - - - - - -	2,200
Highbury - - - - - -	1,785
Liverpool - - - - - -	1,616
City of London - - - -	1,473
Newcastle - - - - - -	1,130
Bromley - - - - - -	1,046
Brighton - - - - - -	1,020
Sheffield - - - - - -	1,015

(Liverpool supporters please note that 766 off-street meters are included in the total).

Second Division

Croydon	1,000
Bristol	997
Redbridge	880
Worthing	842
Southend	824
Lambeth	770
Hull	726
Southwark	680
Sutton	680
Hammersmith	675
Brent	650
Wolverhampton	622
Kingston	570
Harrow	520

Third Division

Hackney	470
Cambridge	450
Merton	450
Richmond	420
Plymouth	396
Havering	360
Luton	310
Maidstone	257
Greenwich	245
Tower Hamlets	180
Banbury	120
Boston	48

Scottish Division

Edinburgh	3,500
Glasgow	2,600

Disappointed 'clubs' whose managers applied to join in 1960 but who had second thoughts include Cardiff, Gloucester, Leicester, Norwich, Walsall, Worcester and York. Among the smaller applicants were Chelmsford, Cleethorpes,

Mansfield, Hinckley and Sutton Coldfield. All of these decided finally to refuse Mr Marples' golden handshake. They deserve congratulation.

Meters: Q and A

It had been the practice, when a parking meter scheme was introduced, for the parking authority to provide a guide in the form of a Question and Answer leaflet for road users. The first was composed in July 1958 for the North-West Mayfair Parking Scheme, Britain's first experiment with the parking meter. It was a list of some 20 Questions, starting with 'What is the area in which meters have been installed?' and ending with the question on everyone's lips 'What will the Council do with any profits from the meter scheme?' The London leaflets were not very lively compositions, but as the meter moved about the country Town Clerks, Borough Engineers and Chief Constables got together and produced more readable efforts. It is a great pity that so many of these

are now out of print because they provide a lot of useful information, all relevant today—except of course that the parking charges have been increased, notably since decimalisation.

The following are some of the Questions and Answers which are correct for all meter schemes in controlled parking zones. They are modelled on the impersonal City of Westminster leaflet with variations suggested by the more personal guides issued subsequently in provincial areas, the Brighton leaflet in particular.

Q: *How do I know when I am in the controlled zone?*

A: 'Zone Entry' and 'End of Zone' signs are sited at all points at which you enter and leave the controlled zone.

Q: *Where can I park?*

A: Only in a metered parking bay.

Q: *Where must I not park?*

A: Streets or parts of streets not marked out as parking places are 'No Waiting' streets. (Note that yellow lines are now mandatory in controlled parking zones).

Q: *What is a parking bay and what is a parking place?*

A: A parking bay is a space marked on the road by white lines with a parking meter alongside. Parking bays are grouped in parking places and the limits of a parking place are indicated by double white lines. Any unmetered spaces are provided for loading and unloading and picking up and setting down passengers. You must not park in these spaces. Most parking bays measure 20 feet in length, but many are shorter. They are for the accommodation of one vehicle only.

Q: *What vehicles may use a parking bay?*

A: Private cars (passenger vehicles constructed to carry not more than 12 persons, exclusive of the driver), goods vehicles, motor cycles (but solo motor cycles, scooters and mopeds have their own free parking areas) and invalid carriages—*but no trailers.*

Q: *For how long may I park and what is the charge?*

A: Consult the meter.

Q : *How do I start the meter working?*

A : Merely by inserting the appropriate coin. There are no handles, buttons or switches to be operated.

Q : *Can I use unexpired time?*

A : Yes, but you must decide when you park how long you intend to stay and if it is longer than the unexpired time you must insert the appropriate coin or coins at the time of parking. You cannot return later to obtain more time. This is meter-feeding and is an offence.

Q : *Having paid for a certain time, may I return later and extend the time by inserting a further coin?*

A : No—this is meter-feeding and is an offence.

Q : *What happens if I overstay the period paid for?*

A : A yellow flag will appear in the meter. When a patrolling traffic warden or parking attendant sees this flag he will place a notice on the vehicle, informing the driver he has incurred an Excess Charge. The vehicle may be left at the meter for the limited excess period shown on the meter. Failure to pay this Excess Charge within seven days is an offence.

Q : *What happens if at the end of the excess period the vehicle still remains at the meter?*

A : The traffic warden or parking attendant will issue a penalty notice in addition to the excess charge notice. The vehicle may be removed to a car pound.

Q : *After leaving a parking bay may I use another bay in a different parking place?*

A : Yes. You may not return to the same parking *place* for one hour but you may park in another parking place immediately.

Q : *What if the meter is officially marked Out of Order?*

A : You may park free of charge provided you remove the car within the maximum time limit on the meter after its repair, ie you are entitled to at least two hours free parking at two-hour meters.

Q : *Will there be any occasions when parking will not be permitted even at a parking bay?*

A : Occasionally it may be necessary to suspend a parking

bay for a special reason. In such cases the meter will be covered with a red hood marked 'Bay suspended. No Waiting. No Loading or Unloading.'

Q : *Outside meter hours is it 'safe' to use a parking meter?*

A : Normally police encourage motorists to use metered parking places after hours. But in London, the Metropolitan police warn that if evening traffic becomes exceptional eg in the vicinity of theatres, police may have to remove cars even though they are at meters.

'No Further Action'

Owner Liability is the 'block buster' designed to relieve the frightful constipation suffered by those whose duty it is to enforce the law of the fixed penalty notice. The remarkable thing is of course that the condition was allowed to persist for so long. Constipation is not serious in the ordinary way but it can become chronic. It can make things most uncomfortable for the sufferer and one would expect that his complaint would be attended to without prolonging the agony. Yet in the case of the fixed penalty notice it went on for all of fifteen hard years, from 1960 to 1975.

Hear what Sir Joseph Simpson, father of the traffic warden, was saying in 1961:

Initial experience has shown that recent provisions designed to simplify the procedure against offenders for minor traffic offences are still too cumbersome. Unless the motoring public show a greater sense of respect for the law, both in conforming to regulations and replying to legally authorised notices, further short cuts will be inevitable.

The Commissioner's colleague in the City of London said, quite bluntly:

Our ticket system for the meters in London is not working because the people who get the tickets don't comply with them. If they didn't comply in America it wouldn't matter because the registered owner of the car would be responsible for the offence, and it would be very easy for the police to issue a summons.

Hear also what Robert Mark, when Chief Constable of Leicester City, had to say in his *Second Thoughts on Parking Meters*:

In the United States and Europe, this procedure is shortened by making the registered owner of the vehicle responsible for such offences if the identity of the driver cannot readily be determined.

These indeed are true sayings and worthy to be believed. By 1967 the Home Office could no longer ignore the call for Owner Liability. They instituted a nationwide survey to identify the grounds on which police prosecutors gave up trying, the cases which were written off, marked No Further Action. It emerged that from a total of 774,274 Fixed Penalty Notices issued in England and Wales during the previous year no less than 25 per cent had been written off.

Drivers entitled to diplomatic privilege - - - -	15,497
Visitors from abroad who have left the UK - - -	42,279
Unable to trace the driver - - - - - -	51,109
Statutory time for proceedings expired - - - -	21,042
Traffic warden resigned or not available - - -	1,191
Mistakes on tickets - - - - - - - - - -	14,739
Cautioned and/or excused payment - - - -	23,311
Other reasons - - - - - - - - - - - -	31,466

There was no complaint over the last two categories. These were cases where police bowels had been moved by compassion. (The large number of 'other reasons' fell almost entirely to the metropolitan police, those sticklers for correct precedure who never issue a caution when they excuse payment. They simply 'withdraw proceedings'.) Nor could much be done about diplomatic privilege. But visitors from abroad were often phonies, nominating a driver with a Paris address, a ploy which owner liability could cope with. It was the 70,000 who escaped because they would not stand up and be counted who were the niggers in the painful pile.

The Commissioner from his throne at New Scotland Yard was getting black in the face. He and his predecessors had been shouting for Owner Liability year after year. The strain was intolerable, as his wretched reports showed. It just went from bad to worse.

	1967	1968	1969
Notices issued	459,849	603,716	810,580
	%	%	%
paid	53.2	45.4	43.0
written off	20.6	29.1	31.9
prosecuted	2.5	1.4	1.1
outstanding	23.7	24.1	24.0

At last, in 1970, ten years too late, things started moving. Parliamentary draftsmen began fashioning a device to insert into the fixed penalty provisions. It came finally to a head when Mr Heath had actually to walk from 10 Downing Street to the House of Commons. The GLC transport chief was living it up in Tokyo at the time. He was summoned back. County Hall called for a £10 ticket. The Commissioner put Owner Liability first. The motoring public jeered. 'Only mugs pay parking fines'.

Mr Heath misjudged the situation and a General Election caused the first Road Traffic Bill to be shelved. It was not until September 1975 that the law was changed. Loud were the noises from Ticket Offices throughout the land. It was Owner Liability—at last!

No Lights

The lighting requirements on stationary vehicles are the same for the entire country. They were greatly simplified in 1972. The rules are now as follows:

1 Motors cars, motor cycles, and vans and lorries not exceeding 30 cwt unladen, when parked on roads subject to a speed limit of 30 mph or a lower speed limit need not show lights, whether or not street lamps are lit, *provided that* no part of the vehicle is within 15 yards of a road junction and the vehicle is parked with its nearside close to and parallel with the kerb.

2 Vehicles above 30 cwt unladen and those constructed or adapted to carry eight or more passengers must have both front and rear lamps lit when stationary on any road during the hours of darkness, ie from $\frac{1}{2}$ hour after sunset to $\frac{1}{2}$ hour before sunrise.

3 Outside a 30 mph speed limit area all vehicles must display two white lights to the front and two red lights to the rear. Single parking lights are not sufficient and it is not legal merely to have side lights on one side of the vehicle.

4 The only exception to parking otherwise than with the nearside of the vehicle next to the kerb is when using a one-way street. Lights are not now required in recognised

parking places, pursuant to The Road Vehicles Lighting (Standing Vehicles) (Exemption) (General) Regulations 1975.

Parking in breach of the lighting regulations carries a possible court fine of £100, but it is a fixed penalty offence and one would expect the normal procedure to be punishment by ticket. This is not the general rule, however. Prosecution policy varies widely. Surrey police prefer court proceedings on every occasion. Sussex police issue fixed penalties, a total of 6,000 in 1975. Police throughout Wales take every offender to court. Merseyside police issued 9,000 tickets against unlit vehicles in 1975. Greater Manchester issued none. In the Metropolitan Police District traffic wardens issued only 51 fixed penalties for lighting offences in 1975 but police issued over 500.

The Magistrates Association does not regard unlit parking as a grave offence. It suggests a tariff of £8 for parking on the wrong side *if the road is lit* and £15 if the road is unlit. A fixed penalty of £6 seems more than adequate if the road is lit. Why trouble the courts when all pleas must be guilty?

Nuisance

The parked car can be a great nuisance. Some might say it is a public nuisance. Certainly to residents and to frontagers generally the car which obstructs the common law right of access to one's own premises is a confounded nuisance, but one which, in legal terms, can be 'abated'. The complainant is entitled, within limits, to take the law into his own hands.

There was a case in 1966 which is discussed and reported, without naming the parties, in the *Journal of Criminal Law*. It was the case of a motorist who had parked in a residential street and had returned after two hours to find the car had been moved. The quarter light retaining catch had been broken and a 'glue-like' substance had been spread over the driver's seat. He brought an action alleging wilful damage under s.14(1) of the Criminal Justice Administration Act 1914. The damage claimed was wholly for the window, £7.0.6, nothing for the car seat.

63

The defendant's evidence was that he found the car wholly blocking the exit from his garage. He made enquiries, waited ten minutes, and because he required his own car to attend a business meeting, he pushed open the quarter light and moved the obstructing car. He then returned to his dining room and took marmalade from the breakfast table which he proceeded to spread over the car's front seat. He added that a friend of his had previously dealt similarly with an offending car and had not been obstructed again.

Mr Edward Robey, the stipendiary magistrate, son of a famous comedian, was not amused but he dismissed the case. The obstruction constituted a nuisance. The defendant did no more than was reasonably necessary to remove the nuisance. But there was the question of the marmalade. 'The plaintiff wiped it off and does not claim any damage was caused thereby, which is fortunate from the defendant's point of view, because had he, in temper, slashed the seat and done such sort of damage he would have had no answer.' The incident of the marmalade was, however, severable.

A more common form of reprisal is to let down the offender's tyres. There is, however, no question that this is a criminal activity. It is certainly conduct likely to occasion a breach of the peace. It may be arguable whether it involves theft of air, but it can certainly involve a charge of criminal damage to both the tyre and the rim while to unscrew the valve is surely 'tampering' under section 29 of the Road Traffic Act 1972, for which the penalty can be a fine of £100:

> If, while a motor vehicle is on a road or on a parking place provided by a local authority, a person otherwise than with lawful authority or reasonable cause gets on to the vehicle or tampers with the brake *or other part of its mechanism,* he shall be guilty of an offence.

There remains the old common law offence of Nuisance, still available but only by indictment:

> Obstruction of the highway is a species of Nuisance to be found in many places and is fit to be suppressed. The primary object of the street is for the free passage of the public and anything which impedes that free passage is a Nuisance.

Lord Ellenborough CJ returned to the theme in 1812 (R v Cross 3 Camp Rep 224) when he made his famous observation 'No one can make a stableyard of the King's Highway'.

No one? He little reckoned with what Ernest Marples and the parking meter would do in 1960. Lord Marples will have a lot to answer for when he meets up with Lord Ellenborough on the Day of Judgment.

Obstruction
Parking in Britain is bedevilled by antiquated law. This was the conclusion of the Royal Commission on the Police in 1962:

No law can be considered satisfactory unless it commands wide popular support and its purpose is understood and accepted. We do not think that the present provisions of the law with regard to the parking of motor vehicles satisfies either test . . . We recommend that the law be reviewed, simplified and modernized so that any driver will know where he may and may not park his vehicle without committing an offence.

The law under criticism was made in 1835 and in 1904. It is the law which punishes obstruction by stationary vehicles. The offence of Wilful Obstruction was created by the Highway Act 1835 and it is repeated in the Highways Act 1959. The offence of causing Unnecessary Obstruction was created by the Motor Cars (Use and Construction) Order 1904, made by the Local Government Board on the passage of the Motor Car Act 1902. The identical provision is repeated in the Motor Vehicles (Construction and Use) Regulations 1973. It is a case of old wine in new bottles. The labels are different but it has the same sour taste.

'These provisions', said the final report of the Royal Commission, 'have been interpreted by the courts from time to time, but they cause much confusion and doubt in the minds of motorists and leave much discretion to the police. This is not a satisfactory solution.'

'Wilful Obstruction' is no problem. 'It depends on all the circumstances including the length of time the obstruction continues, the place where it occurs, the purposes for which it is done, and, of course, whether it does in fact cause an actual as opposed to a potential obstruction.' (Lord Parker in Nagy v Weston 1965 1WLR 280). Wilful Obstruction is inexcusable. But police do not often use it against the private motorist: it tends to be reserved for sellers of hot dogs and obstinate chauffeurs.

'Unnecessary Obstruction' was a purpose built offence, created for the motor car. It formed part of regulations which were considered basic in 1904, some of which have stood the test of time and are law to this day, eg as to the driver being in such a position as to have proper control and also limiting

66

the distance he should travel in reverse—all sensible stuff. But 'unnecessary' obstruction was something to be viewed subjectively or objectively. The motorist was always at a disadvantage because the evidence was of something that had happened in his absence. If police said 'traffic was reduced to a single alternate line' there could be no argument. But it was generally agreed that 'actual', not 'potential', obstruction was the criterion.

In 1956 a barrister, Mr Peter Solomon, for whom there was no room in his Inn, left his car on what was then the widest carriageway in the whole of London, the Thames Embankment, where there were three lanes for traffic in each direction. Unluckily he parked on the City of London area and though Metropolitan Police might not have objected a City police officer reported his car, along with others, for standing in line for over five hours. No actual obstruction was alleged but it was claimed to be 'unnecessary' because others might have wished to park there for shorter periods. The learned City Alderman who at that time sat as the sole judge imposed a fine of £2. The barrister appealed. The Alderman gave as his reason for the conviction his opinion that five hours parking was an unreasonable use of the highway. In the Divisional Court Lord Goddard CJ was very scathing. He was sure

that **Mr Solomon** wanted to help his profession as well as motorists by raising high juristic principles, but his Lordship was bound to say that it raised nothing but a pure question of fact.

> I entirely fail to see how it can be said that a stationary car is not an obstruction on the highway; it certainly is, because it obstructs the free passage. One cannot walk over or drive over a place where a stationary car is standing, but such are the exigencies of modern life that no one is going to say that leaving a car for a reasonable time is an obstruction sufficient to make it an offence. Therefore, the regulations in question in this case have been careful to make it an offence, not merely to obstruct, but to cause unnecessary obstruction. If a car, or a barrel, or a fence—because there is work going on—is in the road, that is an obstruction. A car becomes an unnecessary, or may become an unnecessary, obstruction if it is left there too long, and the alderman thought that in this case there was an unnecessary obstruction because it was unreasonable. If it was unreasonable, it follows that it was unnecessary. (Solomon v Durbridge 1956 JP 231).

The AA has bitterly regretted its support for **Mr Solomon**. The case, though never cited in the regular law reports, soon leaked out and it has been seized on hungrily by police. It provided a stick to beat any motorist who parked for an 'unreasonable' time. Whole streets could be blitzed, including cars parked by residents. Only a resolute magistracy could control such a situation. Such was the bench in Oswestry which decided that one and a quarter hours parking, albeit on market day, was not 'unreasonable'. Lord Widgery rejected the police appeal. The question of 'unnecessary' obstruction was purely one of fact in every case. He would not upset the Oswestry finding. (Evans v Barker 1971 RTR 453).

Where does this leave the motorist? What is this thing called 'obstruction'? Traffic wardens can't tell you. They are not taught obstruction law. The offence had been repidly removed from the jurisdiction of the fixed penalty ticket. It was considered 'too controversial'. You can say that again!

Offences

I *Obstruction Offences*

Obstruction offences are expressly excluded from the £6 Notice of Opportunity to pay a Fixed Penalty system. They are as follows. with the maximum fine. They are not subject to either disqualification or endorsement.

1	Unnecessary obstruction contrary to the Construction and Use Regulations 1973	£100
2	Wilful obstruction contrary to the Highways Act 1959	£50
3	Wilful obstruction contrary to the Town Police Clauses Act 1847 or the Metropolitan Police Act 1839	£20 or 14 days imprisonment

II *Waiting Restrictions*

The following are waiting offences specified in fixed penalty notices. They are all infringements of prohibitions or restrictions imposed under the Road Traffic Regulation Act 1967 or under local enactments or byelaws. The maximum court fine in every case is £100.

1 The vehicle was waiting in a restricted street/a restricted or prohibited road/a scheduled street or road/in a part or length of a restricted street or road/or in an area where waiting is restricted or prohibited.

2 The vehicle was used on a road prohibited to such a vehicle/being a commercial vehicle was used in a restricted street.

3 The vehicle was loading/unloading in a prohibited area or was waiting to deliver or collect goods when waiting for such purpose was then prohibited.

4 The vehicle was waiting on that side of a road on which waiting was prohibited on that day.

5 The vehicle was waiting on that side of a road on which waiting was permitted on that day for a period longer than that permitted.

6 The vehicle was waiting on a prohibited road—a clear-

69

way / the vehicle was stationary on the carriageway of a street where vehicles were prohibited from stopping—a clearway.

7 The vehicle was stationary on a cab rank.

8 The vehicle was stationary on a bus stop.

III *Parking Place Regulations*

The following are the offences liable to be committed at parking places controlled by parking meters, as specified on fixed penalty notices. The maximum court fine is £20.

1 The vehicle was left in a parking place, the initial charge not having been duly paid.
2 The vehicle was left in a parking place for more than the permitted period after the excess charge was incurred.
3 The vehicle was left in a parking place before the expiration of one hour after it had been taken away from a parking bay in that parking place.
4 The vehicle was of a class or description of a vehicle not authorised to be left in the parking place.
5 The vehicle was waiting in a parking place elsewhere than in a parking bay or parking space.
6 The vehicle was waiting in a parking place where a hood over a meter indicated that use of the bay was suspended, or a traffic sign indicated that waiting by vehicles was prohibited.
7 The vehicle was waiting in a parking place where a traffic sign indicated that waiting by vehicles was prohibited.
8 The vehicle was improperly parked in a parking place: every part of the vehicle was not within the limits of the parking bay.

Parks Regulation Acts 1872 and 1926
1 The vehicle was parked in contravention of a notice or sign exhibited by order of the Secretary of State.
2 The vehicle was left unattended elsewhere than in a place for the time being appointed for the purpose.

Residents Parking Permit Offences
The vehicle was waiting in a parking place where there was a traffic sign 'Permit Holders Only'/'Card Holders Only' without there being displayed on the vehicle a valid permit/parking card/the document requiring to be displayed or without payment of the charge being indicated by a token affixed to a valid permit/parking card displayed on the vehicle or by the display of a valid season ticket or daily ticket.

IV *Highway Code Offences*
In addition to Obstruction, Waiting and Parking offences there

are the ten commandments: the musts and must-nots listed in the Highway Code. The maximum court fine for each offence is the same, £100 plus certain endorsement and possible disqualification for the pedestrian crossing offence, for dangerous parking and for parking opposite double white lines.

1 When you stop you *must* set the brake and stop the engine before you leave the vehicle.
2 You *must* switch off your headlamps at night, but leave your side and tail lights on unless unlit parking is allowed.
3 You *must not* stop your vehicle on the approach side of an uncontrolled Zebra crossing or Pelican crossing beyond the double line of studs in the road or stop in the Zebra controlled areas which are marked by a pattern of zig zag lines on either side of an uncontrolled Zebra crossing, nor within the limits of any type of pedestrian crossing.
4 You *must not* park your vehicle or trailer on the road in such a way that it is likely to cause danger to other road users.
5 You *must not* park at night on the right-hand side of the road (except in a one-way street).
6 You *must not* park on the footway unless authorised.
7 You *must not* park opposite a double white line central road marking.
8 You *must not* open any door of your vehicle so as to cause injury or danger to anyone.
9 You *must not* stop in a bus lane during prohibited hours.
10 On a motorway, you *must not* stop on the carriageway or on the central reserve and you must not stop on the hard shoulder or verge except in emergency.

V *Miscellaneous Offences*
1 Any contravention of a parking places order (eg meter feeding or failure to pay an excess charge) £20
2 Interference with a parking meter, operating it or attempting to operate it by the insertion of objects other than current coins of the appropriate denomination with intent to defraud £50

3 Tampering with a ticket machine with intent to defraud or using false coins or other objects   £50

4 Plying for hire or accepting passengers for hire while a vehicle is within a parking place   £20

5 Removing or interfering with a fixed penalty notice or excess charge notice except by or under the authority of the driver or person in charge of the vehicle or the person liable for the offence in question   £20

6 Forgery or alteration of a ticket issued by a machine, using or lending a ticket or allowing it to be used, with intent to deceive   £200

7 Knowingly making a false statement to procure the issue of any authorisation   £200

8 Failure to furnish information as to the identity of a driver unless a court is satisfied that the defendant did not know and could not with reasonable diligence have discovered his identity   £50

9 Failure without reasonable excuse to furnish a statutory statement of ownership   £100

10 Recklessly or knowingly furnishing a false statement of ownership   £400

VI *Dumping of Vehicles*

By s.19(1) of the Civic Amenities, 1967, any person who without lawful authority, abandons on any land in the open air, or on any other land forming part of a highway, a motor vehicle or anything which formed part of a motor vehicle and was removed from it in the course of dismantling the vehicle on the land, is liable to a fine of £100, and on second or subsequent conviction to a fine of £200 or three months imprisonment or both.

Owner Liability: Q and A

When Owner Liability was introduced the Metropolitan Police Central Ticket Office issued a leaflet of nine questions and answers:

Q : *What is 'owner liability'?*

A : Owner liability means that the owner of a vehicle may be liable to conviction of an offence for which a Fixed Penalty Notice has been issued but the fixed penalty not paid, even though he was not the driver when the offence was committed.

Q : *How and when was 'owner liability' introduced?*

A : By Sections 1 to 5 of the Road Traffic Act 1974 with effect from 1st September 1975.

Q : *Who is the 'owner'?*

A : The owner will in most cases be the person in whose name the vehicle is registered and whose name appears in the log book or registration document. It will, therefore, be in the interest of vehicle owners to ensure that the registration authority is notified promptly of any change of ownership. It is also a separate offence to fail to notify such a change forthwith.

Q : *How will the owner know of his liability?*

A : If he himself was the driver at the time he should know about the issue of the Fixed·Penalty Notice or the driver may have informed him, but in the absence of payment of the fixed penalty he will be sent or given a Notice to Owner of Vehicle, or, if he has been named as hirer by a vehicle firm, a Notice to Hirer of Vehicle.

Q : *What will the Notice say?*

A : It will give details of the alleged offence for which the Fixed Penalty Notice was issued, the serial number of the Fixed Penalty Notice, directions for payment of the fixed penalty with a payment slip and notes for guidance on how to comply with the Notice.

Q : *What will happen if the Notice is ignored?*

A : The recipient of the Notice may be prosecuted for failing to comply with the requirement in the Notice and upon conviction the maximum penalty is £100.

Q : *What must be done when a Notice is received?*

A : If the fixed penalty is paid in the way described in the Notice nothing further need be done, otherwise in order to comply with the Notice the person *must* make a

74

statement confirming or denying ownership at the time of the parking offence to which it relates to the effect that: —

(a) he was the owner at that time, or

(b) he ceased to be the owner before that time, or

(c) he became owner after that time, or

(d) the vehicle is not one which he has owned.

If (b) or (c) applies, he should give particulars of the person (or company, firm or other authority) to whom he transferred the vehicle or from whom he acquired it. The statement as to ownership should be made on the space provided on the Notice and the form returned to the Central Ticket Office within 14 days.

Q : *What if someone else was driving at the time?*

A: In addition to the compulsory statement of ownership, a statement about who was driving may also be given by the owner but to be valid and acceptable it must be signed by both the owner and the person named as driver. In these circumstances the person named as driver may be prosecuted for the traffic offence instead of the owner. If the person named as driver is not prosecuted, because he has left the country for example, then the owner's liability to prosecution remains.

Q: *How will the owner's liability be discharged?*

A : By (a) payment of the fixed penalty by any person, or (b) conviction of any person (driver or owner) for the original traffic offence, or

(c) conviction of any person for failing to comply with the relevant Notice.

There is an additional liability to conviction if a false statement as to ownership or the identity of the driver is knowingly or recklessly furnished. The maximum penalty on conviction of this offence is £400.

But these suggest a further nine questions, based on practical experience of how the law works and the questions which continue to be asked :

Q: *Is there a time limit for proceedings?*

A : Yes. The Notice must be served within six months of the date on which the fixed penalty or excess charge notice was given or affixed. (But in the event of false information the time limit for a prosecution is three years.)

Q: *How are Notices served?*

A : The law says that a Notice may be served either by delivering it to the person to be served or by leaving it at his proper address (a person's 'proper address' being his last known address), or by sending it to him by post. Recorded Delivery is usual but not essential; note that even with Recorded Delivery 'the Post Office does not undertake to deliver to the addressee in person'.

Q: *Is postal service always sufficient?*

A : Yes. The rule is that service is deemed effective by proof of properly addressing, prepaying and posting. Service is deemed to have been effected at the time at which the letter would be delivered in the ordinary course of post.

Q: *What if the Notice is not received?*

A: Ignorance, due to a change of address or for any other reason, may be a 'reasonable excuse' for failing to furnish a statement of ownership.

Q: *What is an owner's 'proper address'?*

A: The law says that a person's proper address is his last known address, ascertained from vehicle registration records.

Q: *What if the registered name or address is wrong?*

A: The law says the owner shall be taken to be the person by whom the vehicle is kept and for the purpose of determining who was the owner at any time it shall be presumed that the owner was the person in whose name the vehicle was at that time registered. So there is a presumption that the vehicle records are correct.

Q: *Must any addressee of a Notice comply with it?*

A: Yes. There is provision in the Notice for every contingency. It must not be returned uncompleted with a covering letter of explanation. This can lead to prosecution for failure to comply and to conviction unless a reasonable excuse is accepted by the court.

Q: *Must details of a transfer be given?*

A: If a person was not the owner at the relevant time he can exonerate himself completely by denying ownership. This statement is not always acceptable unless he can state from whom he acquired it or to whom he transferred it. The law does, however, state that this must be done 'if the information is in his possession'. If the buyer or seller cannot be identified this should be explained.

Q: *What if the real offender will not co-operate?*

A: If an owner cannot persuade the actual driver to pay up, he—the owner—is liable to prosecution and conviction unless he chooses to pay up himself. It is no defence to say that the form of Notice was complied with but the real offender failed to countersign the statement of facts.

Pardons

There seem to be two police schools of thought in this delicate business of pardoning the ticket holder. The hard liners are those whose only answer is 'tell it to the magistrates.' The more liberal police school will conduct almost a trial within a trial before deciding on a prosecution. The ticket holder will never know to which school the ticket office belongs but this should not deter him. The fact is that up to 6 per cent of all fixed penalty notices do result in 'Payment Excused. Offender Cautioned'. This was proved from the Home Office statistics published in 1968 and from current police reports it remains true to this day. The quality of mercy is not strained. It drops on around 100,000 ticket holders every year.

This is the feature of our system, that it is not a fine-on-the-spot but is the offer of an opportunity to pay a mitigated penalty, an offer which may be the subject of review within 21 days or indeed at any time before proceedings are instituted, ie a summons issued. The traffic warden is often obliged to strike in the dark. Had he known all the circumstances he might not have acted. But every fixed penalty notice carries an address for correspondence, not that ticket offices wish to encourage complaints but rather to avoid the wounded writing to the wrong office. Thames Valley police are among the most explicit. 'Any letter in mitigation in respect of the issue of this Fixed Penalty Notice must be addressed to the Chief Superintendent and *not* to the Clerk to the Justices. Any complaint should be forwarded to the same address.'

'Any letter in mitigation'? This appears at once to encroach on the function of magistrates. It conflicts with the hard-line policy dictated by sponsors of the original Bill to introduce fixed penalties. Reference to Hansard will show (HL 1960 vol 224 col 1051) that chiefs of police were not expected to fail in their duty to prosecute. Only 'some extraordinary breach of procedure'—or possibly the discovery that the vehicle had broken down or that the driver was ill—could justify a decision not to prosecute if the penalty remained unpaid. The Metropolitan Police are the only force literally to observe this. The London CTO rendered a nil return to

the Home Office on the number of offenders 'cautioned and excused payment'—but all the same they withdrew over 23,000 tickets for reasons other than diplomatic privilege or because the driver was a visitor from abroad who had left the country. The 'Met' heart is a hard one to soften, but it is not entirely without compassion.

All police ticket offices try to be fair. It is just that some succeed better than others. London withdraws only 3 per cent of its tickets. The West Midlands caution over 6 per cent. Comparisons are odious. In every case the disappointed get a courteous answer. The enquiry has always 'received careful consideration', and this is not belied by the use of a printed form of letter. 'If the fixed penalty is not paid the case will have to be submitted for the adjudication of the magistrates.'

The ticket holder shows a blind faith in British justice when he exercises his prerogative to a court hearing. This again demonstrates the difference between our system and foreign systems. Ours is not an appeal against a prescribed fine. Indeed up to 1974 magistrates were expected to ignore the issue of a ticket. They should start afresh with an open mind. They should listen to the reasons given for not paying the fixed penalty. The appellant should bring with him to court the correspondence with the ticket office. Justice can still be done. The magistrates can always grant an Absolute— or a Conditional—Discharge, or they can dismiss the case outright.

The appeal to the magistrates—a course fraught with risk— is normally the end of the road. The AA went a step further in the early days when London Sessions reduced several fines but Crown Courts are rarely troubled now with appeals against sentence.

When, under protest, the £6 fixed penalty is paid it is best to charge it up to experience and to forget about it. It will be a remarkable windfall if the money is refunded!

'Parking'

> To *park* in the sense of to deposit temporarily, especially a motor car, is modern but the seeds of it can be found in Shakespeare. 'How are we park'd and bounded in a pale'. True, it there implies inability to get out, but that experience it not unknown to the motorist either. The usage started in America: its acceptance in Britain and its extension, often jocular to things other than cars has been whole-hearted. Hats and coats are now *parked* at least as often as they are *left* or *deposited* and the OED Supplement gives examples of its use for deposits varying from children to chewing gum. (Fowler's *Modern English Usage* 1970).

The usage in America derives from the use to which gun parks laid out in the broad streets of Washington were put around 1871.

'Parking' may have progressed from the vernacular to Standard English but it is too imprecise to be recognized by the law, save in the context of 'a parking place', the term being first used in the Public Health Act 1925 to authorise 'parking places'. The act of 'parking' is arguable. There can however be no argument over the vehicle seen 'waiting', 'standing' or 'stopping'. The law of the yellow line is concerned with *'waiting'* offences.

The term 'parkers' is not often encountered but researchers for the new OED Supplement have mined a quotation attributed to no less a person than Lord Marples when he was reported in 1959 as follows:

> Mr Marples gave an example of the immunity these all-day parkers have enjoyed (and still enjoy outside the pink zone) when he described how his manicurist, who parked her old car regularly near Piccadilly, complained to him one day that some other motorist had taken 'her place'.

'Parkers' is an offensive expression but then parking can be offensive. It can be an offence against the environment. PO or the parking offence is something not even your best friend would point out, only that notorious nosey-parker, the traffic warden. By happy coincidence the name of the judge who sat on all the parking cases from 1958 to 1971 was Parker—Lord Chief Justice Parker, of Waddington. All that is post-Parker is sheer Widgery.

Pedestrians

In the calendar of crime 'neglect of pedestrian rights' figures at around 30,000 offences a year. Curiously neglect of regulations governing pedestrian crossings by *stationary* vehicles exceed those by *moving* vehicles, but then stationary vehicles are the easier targets.

New-look Zebra Pedestrian Crossings were introduced in 1971, the new feature being the zig-zag marking on both sides of the crossing. The extension of the parking prohibition to the exit side was made, in the words of the Ministry, to keep the sight lines at crossings clear in both directions, so that drivers and pedestrians can see each other clearly . . . The presence of parked vehicles immediately by the exit side of the crossing detracts from this clear view and can mask approaching pedestrians, particularly on a narrow carriageway. Furthermore, to omit the zig-zags on the exit side would mean that the message to pedestrians, not to cross on the marked areas either side of the crossing would be lost. Research has shown that these areas are very dangerous for pedestrians.

Parking the vehicle *or any part thereof* on the zig-zag lines is an endorsable offence and can rank for totting up. There is no opportunity to escape prosecution by payment of a fixed penalty. The car can be towed away.

The only obligation on a pedestrian is not to loiter on the

crossing. 'No pedestrian shall remain on the crossing longer than necessary to cross with reasonable dispatch.' (Maximum fine £50.)

Jaywalkers are a pest. A jaywalker is of course a pedestrian who will not use pedestrian crossings when these are provided. They tend to get quite out of control in urban areas despite section 23 of the Road Traffic Act 1972 whose enforcement is now extended to traffic wardens, and for which there can similarly be a fine up to £50.

> Where a constable in uniform is for the time being engaged in the regulation of vehicular traffic in a road, a person on foot who proceeds across or along the carriageway in contravention of a direction to stop given by the constable, in the execution of his duty, either to persons on foot or to persons on foot and other traffic, shall be guilty of an offence.

As for pedestrian operated traffic lights, successive Ministers have tried and failed to produce a foolproof system. Barbara Castle's baby born in 1967 was the illuminated white cross which only piled chaos upon confusion. Then there were the matchstick men. 'Unfortunately', said the Ministry, '40 per cent of jaywalkers gave false names and addresses so the scheme didn't really work out.' Matchsticks were replaced by Pelican crossings in 1973. The motorist sees a red, green or flashing amber. The pedestrian sees red, green or a green flashing man. No one is really sure of his flashing rights.

Older motorists still call the yellow globes at zebra crossings 'Belisha beacons', after the Transport Minister who first introduced them. No other Minister is so well remembered. Apart from Ernest Marples their names are forgotten, but for the record they can be recalled to the tune of 'Widdicombe Fair'—Harold Watkinson, Tom Fraser, Barbara Castle, Richard Marsh, Fred Mulley, John Peyton, Old Uncle John Gilbert and all. The newly appointed Will Rodgers has yet to make his name as Secretary of State.

'Scofflaws'

In America they call a person who defies a ticket a 'scofflaw'.

They can get very rough in New York with scofflaws. City marshals scour the streets. They impound cars until fines are paid. New York plates present no problem but now the city is turning its attention to out of state registrations, thanks to the efficient Datacom Collection Systems Inc. Last year the Violations Bureau found a 1973 Cadillac with New Jersey plates owing $6,245 for 146 outstanding tickets. The owner paid up. It seems too that tipsters who can't bear to see parking violations will turn in offenders. The car is sold if the owner fails to appear. It is all big business, the feature being that registrations will not be renewed. The New York ticket which is in the form of a summons states:

If you fail to plead *within seven days* the right to renew the registration of this vehicle may be *denied* and additional fines and penalties may be assessed. Failure to timely *plead*

or *appear* at a hearing will be held to be an *admission of liability* and a default judgment may be entered.

Scotland Yard is green with envy over the New York ticket and God help the British motorist if New York tactics were employed over here. Night courts are held. Courts are not bound by rules of evidence. No more than two adjournments are allowed. Ticket fines increase according to the plea. Failure to accept mail constitutes an admission of liability. It is sheer murder—but they still have scofflaws.

Scotland Yard should forget about New York. They should visit Melbourne, Australia, where the ticket fines are much the same—$4 for a meter offence, $6 for other offences, including the interesting offence of parking in front of a private drive, and $10 for parking on a clearway. But there are few scofflaws in Melbourne. The latest information is that in 12 months 70 per cent of tickets were paid within 14 days. The Town Clerk has reported that from a total of 315,823 reports 229.003 were expiated, producing a revenue of $1,177,086.

'Expiate' must be the clue to Melbourne's success. Their ticket reads:

You may dispose of this matter by either
(a) expiating it by payment of the prescribed penalty, or
(b) having it dealt with by a Court

Then, in red:

If expiating, you have to pay penalty *within 14 days* of date of this notice. Payment, whether posted or delivered, must reach City Treasurer, Town Hall, Melbourne, not later *than fourteenth day*.

The notice concludes:

If you wish to have the matter dealt with by a court, you need take no action on this notice.

On the reverse side is the wording so familiar to holders of the British fixed penalty notice:

85

On payment to the City Treasurer of the prescribed penalty within the period prescribed
(a) the infringement will be deemed to have been expiated,
(b) no further proceedings will be taken in respect of the infringement,
(c) no conviction for the infringement will be regarded as having been recorded.

'Expiating' means to redeem one's sin by payment. In Melbourne the traffic wardens resemble Salvation Army lasses. They issue tickets like copies of the *War Cry* reminding sinners of their opportunity to be saved. Vehicle owners are treated as scapegoats. It is all very uplifting, a holy crusade. We might well follow the Melbourne example. Who knows, many might prefer to 'expiate' their motoring sins.

Six Pounds

The increase in the amount of the fixed penalty from £2 to £6 was a savage blow. If it had been confined to the London area it would have been understandable but to extend it throughout the United Kingdom was most unfair.

The argument for an increase was that £2 was no longer a sufficient deterrent, witnessed by the jump in 1973 of a million more tickets issued than in 1972, when the increase in that year and in 1971 was only half a million. True enough, but this overlooked the fact that London, the Metropolitan Police District, accounted for 70 per cent of these increases. London was knocking up close on 2 million fixed penalties in 1973 and it increased this by 4 per cent in 1974 to reach the grand total of 2,012,335. (All this without reporting a single ticket for non-display of a valid excise licence for which over a quarter of a million tickets were issued in other areas.)

But was an increase to £6 justified even in the London area? In monetary terms the old fixed penalty of £2 in 1960 is worth about £4,95 today. Why not leave it at that? Call it £5 which is exactly what the Magistrates Association recommended. Even on a court hearing prior to 1974 the average fine for a parking offence was £3.60, for lighting offences around £4.15

and for failing to exhibit a licence about £3.75. The fixed penalty is supposed to be *less*, not *more* than a court fine. The Magistrates Association in its recommended penalties has never suggested a 'starting point' for parking offences other than for leaving the car in a dangerous position, zig-zag pedestrian crossing offences and obstruction, for which they recommend fines of £25, £20 and £8 (minimum) respectively. All these are very different from many of the petty offences punished by a fixed penalty.

The trouble is, of course, that there has been a recent overall increase in the maximum fines for all traffic offences and the extent to which a fixed penalty can be raised is geared to the maximum fine for the particular offence. The fixed penalty must not exceed half the maximum fine. The old £2 penalty was related to the maximum fine of £5 for parking place offences. The Road Traffic Act 1974 increased this to £20 while fines for the other fixed penalty offences were increased to £100. The GLC, when consulted, are believed to have opted for a £10 fixed penalty. The AA bid was £4. But the Home Office would not twist. They stuck at £6.

So we have the Fixed Penalty (Increase) Order 1975 which says that the fixed penalty 'shall in all cases be £6.' And here's another grievance. Why must the penalty be the same *in all cases*? Why can't we have a two-tier or a three-tier ticket, as in all other countries? Take the splendid Melbourne ticket, for example. This has a penalty of $4 for an offence at a parking meter; but for leaving the car in a No Standing or a No Parking area, not parallel to the kerb or too far from the edge of the carriageway, on the footway, opposite double lines, double banking, or left within 1 metre of a fire plug or 3 metres of a pillar box and for a host of other specified offences the prescribed penalty is $6. For a Clearway infringement the penalty is $10. (The Australian dollar is worth around 62 pence in our money).

So why can't we have a fixed penalty of, say, £2 for a parking place offence or for failing to exhibit a licence disc? And is not £6 excessive for leaving the car without lights, when the law is never uniformly enforced and is not fully understood, while £6 may just not be enough for deliberately parking on a double yellow line or on a clearway. What is the Home Office objection to such differential treatment? Too complicated for all concerned. 'A single level of fixed penalty has been accepted as appropriate and there seems no clear advantage to be gained from fixing two or more levels of penalty.' This is not good enough. Rumours of a further increase to £10, to appease County Hall, may not be true, but if any such increase is contemplated it must differentiate between the offences to be punished.

Meantime parking offenders must tolerate the £6 penalty. In boxing terms it is a combination punch, a left to the stomach followed by a right to the head, Owner Liability. Ticket holders had been fooling about, holding the ropes, doing an Ali shuffle, mocking the law, not all but too many. It had gone on for fifteen years. The paying customers were beginning to whistle. Traffic wardens were getting disheartened. The referee had to stop the contest. The parking offender cannot now duck the punch. But he can appeal to the magistrates. Was it a fair punch? All he must no longer do is to hold on the ropes.

Stableyards

'The King's Highway is not to be used as a stableyard'. This famous line is from the judgment of Lord Ellenborough CJ in R v Cross (1812) 3 Campbell's Reports, a case of Nuisance on an indictment 'for causing and permitting divers coaches to stand and remain for a long and unreasonable time in the public highway near Charing Cross to the great annoyance of His Majesty's subjects'. It happened in the 52nd year of the reign of George III.

The defendant in R v Cross was the proprietor of a Greenwich stage coach which came to London twice a day. Private carriages were prevented from drawing up conveniently at houses on the opposite side of the road. The prosecution relied on an earlier case, R v Russell (1805), a complaint about wagons, loading and unloading before a warehouse at all hours, when it was held that this was a Nuisance even though there was room for two carriages to pass on the opposite side. 'The primary object of the street is for the free passage of the public and anything which impedes that free passage is a Nuisance . . . This is a species of Nuisance to be found in many other places and is fit to be suppressed'. Counsel for Cross argued that if his client was guilty of Nuisance 'there might be a hundred indictments for the same offence every time a rout is given by a fashionable lady at the west end of the town'. But Lord Ellenborough was not impressed. 'Every unauthorised obstruction of a highway to the annoyance of the King's subjects is an indictable offence'. He repeated, with a nice turn of phrase, 'No one can make a stableyard of the King's Highway'.

It is of interest to note the modern application of this maxim in the celebrated case of Solomon v Durbridge in 1956, when in *The Times* report there was the sub-headline 'Roads treated as Garages'. The Lord Chief Justice, Lord Goddard, a judge with as fierce a reputation as Lord Ellenborough, said that 'many people in London treated the roads as garages'. Said Hilbery J, 'The highway is not a parking place until designated as such'.

But there was not long to wait, for withing 10 years the very place on the Thames Embankment where the unlucky Mr Solomon had parked *was* designated a parking place, with 2-hour parking meters! Lord Ellenborough must have turned in his grave.

Towing Away
There is little humour to be extracted from this macabre subject. It is not funny to lose your car. It is a traumatic experience from which every year, in the West End of London in particular, over 50,000 motorists suffer. It is of course a relief finally to learn that the car is not stolen and that it is awaiting collection at a police station or at a car pound. The poor thing has been arrested. Police, like dog-catchers, have rounded up your car and, as at Battersea Dog's Home, it pathetically waits to be claimed.

One would like to think that police find this towing away

business distasteful. Of course it is in the public interest that cars which cause serious obstruction should be moved. If necessary they should be removed entirely. This was indeed the law until 1968 but since 1968 police do not need to prove 'serious' obstruction. Any obstruction in police eyes will now do, as will any breach of parking prohibitions or restrictions of which a Schedule is attached to the Removal and Disposal of Vehicles Regulations 1968. This Schedule covers legislation from the Metropolitan Police Act of 1839, through the Town Police Clauses Act of 1847, the Burgh Police (Scotland) Act of 1892 on to ten citations from the Road Traffic Regulation Act 1967.

It would really not be going too far to say that any stray

car which is not in an authorised parking place may be removed by the police. Can they possibly enjoy making an example of an offending car by breaking and entering it, leaving the helpless owner distracted by worry and then, the crowning insult, imposing a fixed penalty for the offence involved?

Clearly police ought to find better things to do than taking joy-rides in other peoples' cars. If prevention is the object of the exercise then No Parking signs should at once be erected to warn others from repeating the offence. When this was put to New Scotland Yard the reply was that police had no power to erect temporary no parking signs except in an emergency. Should not TOW AWAY ZONE signs be introduced, as in

America? Would it not suffice if cars were towed away only from double, not from single, yellow lines? And is simple 'obstruction' good enough?

The Metropolitan Police now employ mercenaries to do the dirty work, a team of 50 Vehicle Removal officers, dressed up like security men with VR flashes. They are at home in all makes of car, though some, notably those with thiefproof steering locks, can prove difficult. Limousines, Rolls Royces, Cadillacs? Call up the Z cars, or Z wagons to give them their proper title. Designed by a Mr Jack Breeze of the Yard's Transport Engineers Branch, the Z wagon is claimed to have revolutionized car removal. It has a hydraulic lifting device, using the lifeboat davit technique, to side-hoist vehicles on to a carrying platform, very superior to the old fashioned front lift and tow, a positive boon to any police force in the tow away business. One limousine or two minis can be lifted. (A display for the next Royal Tournament: a Met v West Midlands car lift competition?)

Has the traffic warden any role to play? Traffic wardens are not allowed to remove cars but they can 'cause' cars to be removed. During the last Chelsea Flower Show traffic wardens made hay of cars waiting on yellow lines, calling up the removers to tow away every car in sight, their owners piteously crying along the King's Road for their stolen cars. It is however at the car pound that the traffic warden now has an important role. She will take your money, for the Road Traffic Act 1974 now empowers police to retain custody until the removal fee—lately increased to £15 plus £1.50 per 24 hours storage charge—is paid. This is where possession is indeed nine points of the law. Wardens at car pounds are chosen for their charm, deaf to abuse or entreaties. And this is the one place where a traffic warden can ask to see your driving licence. If the alleged offence is endorsable she can also ask your age, and, if there be any doubt, your sex. She will ask you to sign for the car, and its contents. If junior later complains there is a wrapped sweet missing or madam can't get the driving seat back to its usual position, that's too bad. Actually there are few complaints.

It is ironical that among the most popular of London's car pounds is the one in the Park Lane Underground Garage, rented by police but paid for originally from parking meter profits. This is where payment by credit card—Access, Barclaycard or American Express—is always acceptable, both for removal charges and fixed penalties, a practice for which there is ministry approval.

Traffic Wardens: Abuse and Assaults

Traffic wardens expect abuse, but they are not paid to be assaulted. Mercifully, assaults on wardens do not happen very often. When the Civil Service Union was negotiating a pay rise they claimed that in London the job was a highly dangerous one. Scotland Yard could not agree. There was an element of danger, certainly, and fifteen wardens had been hurt on duty the previous year, the worst case being that of a warden who was attacked with a broken bottle in Camden and needed 21 stitches in a neck wound. Six traffic wardens had been hurt on point duty. 'We are not sure how many of these injuries have been malicious and how many were accidental.' In any event with 1,800 wardens at work at any one time, 15 assaults was minimal.

The courts very properly take a most serious view of an

assault upon a traffic warden. (Merely swearing at a warden is permissible, unless it upsets passers-by.) There was a case in 1972 in the Court of Appeal (Criminal Division) arising from an incident with which wardens are only too familiar. Lord Justice Edmund Davies, as he then was, explained:

What happened was that the appellant parked his car in Duke Street on a yellow line. The vigilant traffic warden, Miss Evans, was about and he told her he was staying there only for ten minutes. She said that he had better find another place, and he answered that his employer's wife was in Selfridges. He was angry. He got out of the car and said 'I'm staying here'. Miss Evans went to his door and said 'Don't be angry, I have a job to do'. He replied 'I'm not getting the sack for you, I'm staying here'. The traffic warden again suggested that he found a different parking place but he insisted on staying. She said there was no alternative for her but to issue him with a ticket. She went

in front of the car to see the registration number. The appellant then drove the car forward quite fast and, before the traffic warden could move, the bumper struck her knees and she fell forward on to the bonnet. At that moment the car braked and she stepped sideways into the road, and this man drove past her laughing. He drove around the block, and on his return said to her 'where the hell do you think I'm going to park?' At this stage the police arrived. This traffic warden was emotionally upset and her right knee was tender. Those are the facts of the case.

For this behaviour the driver was charged with dangerous driving and with assault occasioning actual bodily harm. He

was found guilty and sentenced in the Crown Court to nine months imprisonment, concurrent. A harsh sentence? Not at all. 'By no means wrong in principle.' But the Court of Appeal was disposed to be merciful. The sentence was suspended with the following, not entirely unsympathetic, advice from Lord Justice Edmund Davies:

> Traffic wardens are not in general the pin-ups of the populace. They have frequently exasperating, irritating and sometimes odious duties to perform, but they are duties which in the public interest have to be discharged, and those who find the discharge of a warden's duty personally inconvenient must just put up with it.

He went on:

> The duties of the traffic warden are imposed for the benefit of the public at large, and if it went round that people could treat traffic wardens with the complete disregard this man demonstrated, it would go hard indeed and grave injustice would result. Traffic wardens must be protected and they are entitled to look to the law for that protection.

Traffic wardens get no specific protection. They can look only to the general law, ranging from common assault to

grievous bodily harm. It certainly seems an anomaly that the humble park-keeper gets better protection than the traffic warden. An assault on any park-keeper when in the execution of his duty can result in a sentence of six months imprisonment (*with hard labour* until very recently). Since park-keepers are now 'park police', pursuant to the Parks Regulations (Amendment) Act 1974, the day may soon come when traffic wardens become 'traffic police', if only to obtain similar protection.

Traffic Wardens: 'Affixing'

Every traffic warden must issue a ticket sooner or later. The procedure is carefully taught in the classroom, much as student nurses are taught. The nurse practises her first injections on an orange but the time must come when the syringe is wielded on bare flesh. So it is with the traffic warden. She knows the rules. A Fixed Penalty Notice may be 'given' or it may be 'affixed'. 'A notice affixed to the vehicle shall be deemed to be given to the person liable.'

Traffic wardens do not often need to 'give' a parking

ticket. The gift is not always appreciated. This is when mistakes can be made, because it is difficult to concentrate when the patient is protesting. Some do wait, impatiently; some drive off; some will throw away the gift. (If police are handy this can lead to a prosecution under the Litter Act 1958. 'Defendant did throw down in the open air and there left a Fixed Penalty Notice in such circumstances as to cause the defacement of such place by litter,' for which there can be a fine up to £100.)

There is no set procedure for 'giving' a Fixed Penalty Notice; no formula such as 'I am a traffic warden and I give you this Notice,' touching the offender's person, as with some modes of service. Nor, which is more surprising, is there any procedure prescribed for the Affixing exercise. Traffic wardens are not trained as with the bayonet to step forward smartly and to 'affix' the vehicle. Only in a few areas are there any written Instructions as, for example, in Bristol, where wardens are taught as follows:

Method of issue to motorists
Original (top) copy
The original or top copy is issued to the offender, or where that person is not seen, affixed to the offending vehicle.

When it is not possible to issue the notice to the offender, this copy will be placed in a cleartex bag, sealed with Sellotape and carefully fixed to the windscreen of the vehicle by means of the tape. Under no circumstances will Notices be placed under windscreen wiper blades. If it is not possible to affix the Notice to the windscreen the cleartex bag should be fixed in a prominent position on the offside of the vehicle. In the case of motor cycles the Notice will be attached to the offside twist grip of the machine and not to the petrol tank.

This is 'shipshape and Bristol fashion'—but it is not *de rigueur*. In most areas the mode of affixing is left to the warden's discretion. Their Unions have said they must not be exposed to unnecessary risk. Not only should the procedure not be unduly protracted but lady wardens in particular should not risk injury to themselves by stretching over from the nearside or by stepping into traffic on the offside.

Parking offenders do not care greatly where they are jabbed, but some do rather resent having to peel off yards of sticky tape from the windscreen. Traffic wardens who make such a production number of what should be a simple exercise may have suffered from the gremlins. These gremlins are the people who remove tickets from vehicles which don't belong to them. They have even been known to stick them on adjacent vehicles. There is little proof of this, but it remains a common excuse with some that no ticket was ever issued. It is of no avail. Owner Liability always provides a second Notice of Opportunity.

Traffic Wardens: Functions
In their parking control function traffic wardens have been likened to dog catchers. This is not fair. It is unfair to traffic wardens and unfair to dog wardens. As the lady secretary to the National Dog Rescue Committee wrote in a recent letter to *The Times*: 'The days of the negative dog catcher who sweeps up every available dog into the pound is gone. The dog wardens' policy is to chase the owner as well as the dog . . .' This is indeed the policy, backed by the law, of the traffic warden. And it has been seriously recommended that pursuant to the Justices of the Peace Act 1361 magistrates should consider binding over repeated parking offenders to be of good behaviour and to attend a training course for traffic wardens. Clearly traffic wardens and dog wardens should get together, though dogs need no encouragement to use parking meters.

But traffic wardens have other functions besides dogging the parking offender. This had been their basic function since 1960 but there was a Functions of Traffic Wardens Order in 1965 that presented them with new colours. Police could employ wardens 'in the control and regulation of road traffic at road junctions and at other places, whether on the highway or not, which are or are likely to be congested with traffic, and any other function normally undertaken by the police in connection with the control and regulation of traffic.' Then, in 1970, the two earlier Orders were consolidated and sanction was given to further forms of employment, notably in following up ticket defaulters, in obtaining names and addresses, in working at car pounds and in punishing road fund licence offenders. The Transport Act extended ticket penalties to U-turns and generally gave to wardens total police powers in traffic regulation. Traffic wardens are accordingly a force to be reckoned with. They are proud of their old 1960 motto

'They Shall Not Park', but they have many more useful jobs in the seventies.

Traffic Wardens: Hierarchy
There are 43 chiefs of police in England and Wales, and each chief has his own establishment of traffic wardens. Their quota is temporarily frozen but in any event all are below establishment. The strength of the service in England and Wales, excluding the Metropolitan Police District, at the end

of 1975 was 4,363, a certain increase over the previous year but no higher than in 1973. In the Metropolis the strength at the end of 1975 was 1,830, an increase of a mere 39, recruitment being largely confined to the replacement of wastage.

Traffic wardens are hybrid. They are civilians with police functions. They are controlled by police but they have their own hierarchy. At first there were only 'traffic wardens' but very soon the grade was invented of Senior Traffic Warden or Supervisor. It was in 1970 that there was the Metropolitan outburst of controllers, mastered by Senior Controllers and Area Controllers. By the end of 1975 there were in London 188 Supervisors, 36 Controllers, 17 Senior Controllers and 4 Area Controllers, controlling a total force of 1,585 plain traffic wardens, of whom 1,075 are women. The C-in-C is the Commissioner.

There is no mystery about the function of the 245 men and women who supervise the wardens' activities. They are happy to proclaim themselves in the splendid recruiting brochure *A London Traffic Warden's Job—The Facts you've asked for.*

Let each speak for himself from the pages entitled *The Future as a London Traffic Warden.* (Every traffic warden clearly has a controller's baton in his knapsack.)

Traffic Warden Supervisor
'Mentally it's quite a jump becoming a Supervisor. One moment you were one of the crowd. The next, you've got responsibility for a team. It's to you that other Wardens look for decisions—like whether or not to suspend a certain meter. You help to organise each day for 10—15 Wardens and allocate their beats. Then you make the rounds to check that everything's going smoothly and deal with any small problems that have arisen.'

Traffic Warden Controller
'In this grade you can be second-in-command of a large Warden Centre, or you can be in sole charge of a smaller unit—that's my job. I have 44 Wardens working in my unit which is located in a typically large, widespread and busy suburban area. Organising my wardens and clerical staff in their work, and looking after their welfare is obviously a large part of my job. I handle enquiries from the public. I am consulted about local parking control. If I suggest that double yellow lines should be placed in a certain spot, I'm listened to. It's also my job to organise my wardens to cope with special events, like major football matches.'

Senior Traffic Warden Controller
'I could be in charge of a group of small Warden Centres. As it happens, I control a large unit in the middle of London. Learning how to delegate (and, equally important, assessing correctly to whom to delegate) is vitally important at this level, though the final responsibility for the unit's efficiency is mine, of course. I also organise local training, and liaise with the police over traffic control and parking matters in my area—especially when planning for State Occasions.

Being a *woman* Senior Controller . . .? It makes no difference, though there aren't many of us yet. After all, the

Warden Service ran for 4 years before being thrown open to women, so we've got some time to catch up!'

Area Traffic Warden Controller
'What's so interesting about my job is that I'm in a position to contribute to the overall policy of the Traffic Warden Service. A lot of my time is spent in close liaison with the Chief Superintendent and other senior ranks in the Metropolitan Police Traffic Division. I also deal with correspondence from the public, and sort out problems that have escalated in size for some reason or other. I'm involved in recruiting, too—I sit on selection boards and on boards that determine Warden promotions (I always remember I was a basic grade Warden once). Last but not least, I'm responsible for the efficient deployment of over 600 Wardens. All in all, it's a fulltime job, though a perpetually stimulating one.'

Traffic Wardens: Mark's Gospel

Chief Constable's Office,
Charles Street,
Leicester,
April, 1961.

INSTRUCTIONS TO TRAFFIC WARDENS

1 YOUR PRIMARY ROLE—PREVENTION

You are clearly to understand that your primary function is to help vehicle drivers in streets in the centre of Leicester where waiting is prohibited. You are to do so by:

(i) preventing the unwitting commission of 'waiting' offences; and
(ii) informing vehicle drivers of the parking facilities available to them.

Your efficiency will not be determined by the number of prosecutions you initiate, or by the number of fixed penalty forms you issue, but by the freedom of your patrol area from vehicles parked in contravention of the law.

2 COURTESY

You must always be polite to all vehicle drivers notwithstanding that at times you may feel that you are not accorded by them the civility and co-operation that you are entitled to expect. Remember that many of the people with whom you will deal will have little or no knowledge of the laws relating to parking and waiting. Some of them will have no knowledge at all of their own obligation to avoid causing inconvenience to others and some may consider that their own interests should prevail over those of the public. Try to maintain a courteous attitude notwithstanding that you may be subjected to much provocation. Never invoke for any retaliatory reason the power of enforcement with which you are invested by law. If you decide that it is your duty to invoke it, do so firmly but without departing from the high standard of politeness and good manners expected of a public servant.

3 YOUR SECONDARY ROLE—IMPARTIAL ENFORCEMENT

Your secondary purpose is to enforce the law in respect of waiting offences when you have not been able to prevent them; to that end you must be firm and impartial. You must remember that everyone in this country is equal before the law and that only when faced with a claim for diplomatic immunity need you be concerned about the identity of the person with whom you are dealing. You should invite the claimant to give his name and address and to specify the diplomatic mission to which he belongs. If you act firmly and politely when dealing with vehicle drivers, you are unlikely to give any serious cause for complaint.

These were only the opening paragraphs. The Instructions went on to deal with 'No Waiting', Enforcement, Your Notebook, Disabled Persons, Medical Practitioners, Care of Fixed Penalty Forms and Generally. The entire work was published in 1963 with the title *A Police View on the Control of Parking in Urban Areas.* The author was one Robert Mark, better known today as Sir Robert Mark, Commissioner of Police of the Metropolis, 1972–7.

The background to the necessity for such instructions was the climate of public opinion. Leicester was the first city outside London to be entrusted with the fixed penalty system. It was also the scene of the first revolt against the parking meter. And Leicester was the first to employ women traffic wardens with fixed penalty powers. Leicester did not want a repetition of what was going on in London, where wardens employed to enforce the law of the meter zone were being 'cursed, abused, driven at and swindled'. The Leicester experiment proved a resounding success. The only complaint was from the meter manufacturers.

Sir Robert Mark has been responsible for the largest force of traffic wardens in the country, but he would not cancel one line of what he wrote in 1961 as to the primary rôle of the traffic warden. It is Holy Writ. It is elementary to every police officer in the United Kingdom. It is not the Gospel according to R. Mark, it is police gospel, the gospel of the founding fathers of the regular police. 'A constable's efficiency is not judged by the number of his arrests.' And it is the gospel of the traffic warden also. Some of this may be news to motorists, but it is still Good News.

Traffic Wardens: Mobiles

The London traffic warden service goes from strength to strength. As long ago as in 1972 this is what Sir John Waldron was able to report:

By the end of the year, the traffic warden service had reached a strength approaching the 2,000 mark and had made excellent progress towards achieving self-sufficiency in matters that have hitherto necessitated the involvement of police officers, notably training, supervision and day-to-day operational control. The service has established itself as an indispensable auxiliary arm of the Force, capable of meeting any new demands that may be made of it and flexible enough to adapt to changes in its existing commitments. Traffic wardens are now employed throughout the Metropolitan Police District and they are using vehicles increasingly to reach distant beats and to give mobility to the special teams which provide reinforcement in outlying areas where drivers tend most to ignore 'No Waiting' restrictions. Two more of these teams, making 4 in all, were formed during the year.

The experiment of using a force of mobile wardens had started in 1970, as Sir John had reported the previous year:

The waiting and loading restrictions in controlled parking zones are enforced by traffic wardens, but there are many restricted streets outside the zones where the restrictions are still enforced by foot police. In some areas, owing to other demands on the police, only limited attention has been possible, with the result that drivers have tended to disregard yellow lines and their vehicles have impeded the free flow of traffic and often caused dangerous situations. By way of experiment, 2 small mobile teams of traffic wardens were formed at the beginning of December to enforce waiting restrictions in such areas at the request of the local police.

The Metropolitan Police had made no secret of this. Scotland Yard happily called these their 'flying squads'. 'The squads will be on standby when local police are busy with other matters.' The national press was quick to see the

106

possibilities—'flying wardens', 'dial-a-warden', 'Wardens get Flying Squad'.

Of course it all made sense. Some—possibly the Police Federation who protect police interests or the various unions who protect traffic wardens, may have been suspicious. Could this move to mobility be a foot in the door? Could it infringe the Functions of Traffic Wardens Order of 1970, which, while it enshrined the authority to employ wardens in the control and regulation of traffic and to discharge any other function normally undertaken by police, went on to state categorically that *nothing shall permit these functions to be exercised by a traffic warden who is in a moving vehicle*? No doubt the Home Office had been consulted. Any fears of a mobile force capable of shooting down offenders on the move were ground-less. It was no more than an exercise in moving infantry. Wardens would continue to act *on foot*.

But it did highlight the variety of ways in which traffic wardens could be helpful. It created a Task Force. And it could help recruiting, making an immediate appeal to the younger man or woman willing to volunteer for special duties. In the classroom it could be explained to recruits that this was very similar to the fighter-pilot service in the last war, teams standing by waiting for the order to 'scramble'. Police heli-copters, marked by the AA spotter plane, would be hovering over black spots ready to flash signals to the waiting squads of wardens. To every team—remembering that the age range is 18 to 59—would be added an ex-fighter pilot, for the benefit of his experience and to calm the nerves of the younger wardens as they sped to the scene, their books of fixed penalties at the ready. Sometimes the 'enemy', the black hordes of suburban parking offenders, would get wind of the attack and they would disperse. No matter. A flying warden's efficiency is not judged by the numbers marked up on his vehicle.

Traffic Wardens: Parentage

Parking offenders should be more careful in their choice of language. Traffic wardens are not illegitimate. They may no

longer be able to put their hands on a birth certificate because the Road Traffic and Roads Improvement Act 1960 has now been repealed, but they can point to section 81 of the Road Traffic Regulation Act 1967. This should be enough to satisfy all but the merely abusive.

But there are thoughtful traffic wardens who may be inclined to doubt their status. These are the old hands, the ones who were born in 1960 and who have now reached an age when they begin to ask questions. 'Who am I? Where am I going?' This is a very natural enquiry when you realize that these are not *natural* sons and daughters but persons who have been *adopted*.

It came about like this. One Joseph Simpson, a constable, in his office as Commissioner of Police of the Metropolis, had for years been petitioning the Home Secretary to be allowed to adopt someone to help in what was considered a very unrewarding chore, the control of the motorist. The Home Secretary, a Mr R. A. Butler, consulted colleagues at the

Ministry of Transport, one Harold Watkinson and a certain Ernest Marples. These three gentlemen, all since elevated to the peerage for their services, advised the Queen in Parliament to create persons to be known as TRAFFIC WARDENS. It was pursuant to Section 2 of the Road Traffic and Roads Improvement Act that on 1 September 1960 the message was flashed through the country: *Let there be traffic wardens.* And on the eighth day there was another decree: *Let there be Functions for Traffic Wardens,* and on the 9th day *Let there be Fixed Penalty Orders.* And it was so. And on the 18th day, Monday 19 September, the traffic warden emerged in a corner of London and stung his first parking offender.

There has been a Five Year Plan for the traffic warden, successive Functions Orders until if it were not for the uniform you really could not tell stork (the warden) from butter (the constable). They have equal powers against parking offenders. There should have been another Functions Order in 1975, but instead the warden got as a birthday present on 1 September the Mark 2 Fixed Penalty Notice, the Six Pounder with built-in Owner Liability. (There is a Bus Lane Functions Order promised for the near future).

But not every traffic warden is entirely satisfied. There is still this 'Upstairs, Downstairs' relationship. Father does not come into the kitchen as he used to. The hierarchy is civilianised and Mr Hudson rarely meets the Chief.

Traffic wardens are beginning to realize that others may be making sheeps' eyes at them. County Hall would like to take them over or at any rate to employ them to operate some of their wilder schemes to drive motorists into public transport.

Chiefs have had to appeal to the Godfather of the police, HM Chief Inspector of Constabulary, and in 1973 he issued this warning:

Responsibility for the enforcement of traffic laws and the day-to-day control and regulation of traffic lies firmly within the province of police. It is imperative, therefore, that chief officers of police should continue to have direct control of traffic wardens.

So it is Hands Off our Traffic Wardens. And to the question 'Where am I going?' the answer is 'You're going nowhere—except in police custody.' There is no question of being allowed to leave home. Traffic wardens are not yet of an age to set up on their own.

Traffic Wardens: Recruitment
The temptation to regard traffic wardens as *mercenaries* must be resisted. It is of course true that they are recruited as auxiliaries but not for an emergency operation. The traffic warden service is a career, one for which the recruit must feel a vocation. At the same time money does enter into it. The advertisements in the London press and particularly in magazines which cater for women tried to steer a midway course. In 1970 the payoff was in the last line—*Pay rise pending.*

> Girls! See life as a Traffic Warden in London's glittering West End—and start at £21.37 a week, even as a 19 year old.
> Come and enjoy a job where your everyday world will be famous streets, beautiful shops, elegant squares, historic parks and landmarks of world renown. And people . . . rich and poor, the famous, the unknown, visitors from every continent . . . you'll meet dozens of them in the course of your day, as you control busy pedestrian crossings, advise motorists where to park, direct strangers on the right road and help to keep London's traffic on the move.
> It's an exhilarating life of hustle and bustle, doing responsible, highly interesting work. It's also a job to be proud of. To thousands of visitors this summer, you and other young Wardens are as much a feature of the London West End scene as St. James's Park—and just as attractive.
> Get in touch with us today. Within only a week of applying, you could be starting your training, and earning £21.37 a week.
> *Pay rise pending.*

Then, in 1971:

> 'I'm telling you—it's a super job.' Becoming a Traffic Warden at 19 is something Sharon Goard has never

regretted in two years. 'A friend of mine at the hospital where I worked told me about this job. I used to be shy, but not now—I meet so many people! And I like the hours. I work on Royal routes sometimes. That's a thrill. I never thought I'd see them so close . . . it's a super job! '

I'd like to know more about a Traffic Warden's job in Central London starting at £25.12 a week. I'm aged between 19 and 55.

The results were encouraging, but not sensational. In 1971 the Commissioner reported an increase of 381 wardens but in 1972 the increase was only 89 while in 1973 there had actually been a decrease of 185. Wastage exceeded intake. Something had to be done. The age range was extended and the pay was increased. A stop was put on the girlie advertising and the services of Graham Hill, racing driver, were enlisted. Motorists reduced to strap hangers in London's Underground read with mixed feelings his genial appeal.

'Speed? He could teach me a thing or two' says Graham Hill. 'Traffic wardens have got London's traffic flowing quicker than ever before—even though there's a lot more traffic about. They're definitely in the speed business. Come on and join them. Aged 18 to 59? Call Graham Hill on 230 3717.'

The Graham Hill campaign produced good results. There was, so the Commissioner reported, 'a pronounced upsurge in recruitment and decline in wastage.' It was, as he said, extremely bad luck that there should be this economic freeze on further growth. The rate of pay was no longer the problem, the current starting salary for the Central London warden working within 4 miles of Charing Cross being now over £2,300 a year. (Supervisors can get up to £2,840, Controllers £3,145, Senior Controllers £3,550 and Area Controllers after three years rising to £4,185.)

So why, as the London advertisements were saying in 1976, 'if the job's so good, why are you still advertising for Traffic Wardens when there's so much unemployment?' Came the immediate reply, 'Good question. And here's the even better answer. The plain truth is that so many of the applications we receive are just not good enough to meet our high standards. To be a London traffic warden, you've got to be in good health, with no physical handicaps: have an acceptable weight/height ratio, a good work record, intelligence and an aptitude for the work.'

The London motorist should feel flattered that his parking problems are entrusted to persons of such high calibre. It should be reassuring, too.

Traffic Wardens: Selection

From the host of applicants the candidates selected for interview may not be numerous. It is a waste of time interviewing people who are unlikely to match up to the proper image. In the days before it was considered necessary to be advised by management consultants the Metropolitan Police had been quite blunt about the priorities. In answer to the question 'As a traffic warden, what would I do?' there was the answer 'You would have to enforce the law relating to parked vehicles and assist in the control or regulation of traffic as required. You would have to issue penalty tickets when offences were committed, but you would also be there to advise and assist the public in many ways, too. The work is full of interest and easy to learn. You are not confined to an office or factory and you enjoy security and good companionship, doing a vitally important job.'

The applicant was left under no illusion as to the type of person preferred. 'Give details of any service in HM Services, the Merchant Navy, the Special Constabulary, the Territorial Army etc.' He was asked also to attach 'a short statement (50—80 words) in your own handwriting, saying why you would like to be a traffic warden.'

Whether from choice or necessity the London traffic warden of today hardly fits the image of the sixties. In the regions, however, the old appeal still applies. The warden is a traffic policeman, recruited to enforce severe restrictions. Local authorities may want to strangle the city centre, to throw a *cordon sanitaire* against infection by vehicles, with mazes of

traffic directions, traffic lights set at red, no entry here, turn left there, stop, give way, get out, abandon cars, enter public transport. It is no job for the lightweight. There is a war situation. Town centres must be cleared of all but essential traffic. Private motorists have to understand there is a curfew, a strict order that no vehicle may be seen on a yellow line on pain of summary punishment. Regional wardens in strictly controlled zones do not fraternize as in London. They are not hostile but they are there to enforce the law, to discipline as much as to educate.

The services take recruits where they can be found but there is time to subject them to rigorous training before they are sent into action. It will be two years before your police cadet is entrusted with a truncheon. The traffic warden gets only a few weeks in the classroom and less than that under tuition on the street. Scrupulous selection by the appointments board is essential. The qualities expected are 'aptitude, intelligence and capacity for responsible work'. 'Healthy, active, outward-going men and women, between 18 and 59' are required in London. Police know the right type at a glance. An Assistant Commissioner (Traffic) once said he wanted people 'who know what life is all about'. Good deportment, clear handwriting, strong legs, common sense. Health? 'You're out in all weathers. It's not a job for the molly-coddled'. Self-confidence. 'You have authority, but you're expected to wear it lightly. Calmness laced with firmness is what we look for.'

Really it is hardly surprising that, as the advertisement says, 'Traffic Wardens—many apply but few are chosen'.

Traffic Wardens: Sex Discrimination

Traffic wardens are persons employed to discharge functions normally undertaken by the police. Now, so far as is known, it has never been 'normal' for women police to perform traffic duties. Why this should be is difficult to understand, there being a total strength of over 4,000 regular women constables in England and Wales, not to mention a further 500-odd senior ranks. But traffic, which includes parking, seems always to have been a man's job. However, women's liberation arrived in 1960. All over the country enlightened chiefs of police began to recruit women as traffic wardens.

But like the call to arms in 1914 which took three years to be heard in America it took just about that time before the greatest army of traffic wardens ever to be formed—that of the Metropolitan Police—recruited a single woman. The Commissioner had been so taken aback by the reception given to his initial force of 60 virgin soldiers, all male and very mature, that he could not bring himself to recognize the successes of mixed bags of wardens in other parts. Leicester City had blazed the trail in 1961, not that Mr Mark attributed his success entirely to the 20 ladies who shared the experience with an equal number of men. But they were there to be seen and to be photographed. They were the last word in deportment, and Leicester City was very regimental at that time: saluting drill was on the training syllabus. Indeed, all training and disciplines were on police patterns. There appeared no reason why women should not share with men the duties of a traffic warden. But the idea was not universally favoured and it was only when Scotland Yard finally surrendered that women became generally acceptable.

The position today is that outside the London area male traffic wardens marginally outnumber female by 2,205 to 1,835. There are bright spots—in Cheshire, for example, where 65 out of 68 wardens are women—while in the areas which include the big cities women do get proportionately better representation, 136 women to 86 men in Greater Manchester, 190 women to 48 men in the West Midlands. But there are still areas which are a disgrace—Northumbria with 116 men to 35 women, Sussex with 133 men to 47 women. The real chauvinist pigs hide away in Devon and Cornwall (152 men to only 10 women) and in Norfolk, with its 2 solitary women to 51 men.

In Scotland, by the very nature of the job which must take into account the need to work in pairs due to Scots law of corroboration, you would not expect to find women; but they are there, 292 women to 522 men. In a recent report HM Chief of Scottish Constabulary was obviously pleased to report on the success of women. They had shown 'particular aptitude . . . their smartness had impressed me on numerous occasions . . . many women wardens with grown up families find the work congenial . . . an interesting outdoor life . . .'

But of course it is in London, in the service of the Metropolitan Police, that women are now pre-eminent. The basic traffic wardens outnumber the men by 2 to 1: 1,075 women to 510 men. Whether it is from choice or necessity the call today is for women, and in some areas men need not apply. One London newspaper advertisement (before the Sex Discrimination Act) can speak for itself:

Ladies—make the Marble Arch area part of your life! Get to know the area like an expert. Not only Marble Arch but Edgware Road, Oxford Street, Little Venice, St. John's Wood, Baker Street. Get to know the people who live there, work there, and travel in and out of the area. Advise them on parking regulations, control the traffic at busy intersections, and keep the cars and buses flowing smoothly in one of the busiest parts of London. Make it part of your life—and earn over £2,000 a year for doing a secure job. Be a Traffic Warden. There are vacancies now. (September 1975).

There are indeed vacancies and not only in the Marble Arch area. There are vacancies throughout the traffic warden service. On 31 May 1975, replying to a series of questions on police recruiting and wastage, Dr Summerskill gave statistics that showed the traffic warden service in England and Wales to be 3,000 short of establishment—a total of 6,211 against an authorised establishment of over 9,000, with the Metropolitan force the hardest hit:— 1,841 against an establishment authorised of 2,967, which was still far short of what the Commissioner had said were his requirements. The unkindest cut has been the freeze imposed on personnel paid wholly or partly from the rates.

But motorists ought not to rejoice over any shortage. What we want is not fewer but more traffic wardens, preferably taken off parking duties and preferably female. We are not masochists but if there is to be any punishment many find it more bearable from feminine hands.

Traffic Wardens: Training

> A police authority shall not employ as a traffic warden any person who is a constable, but shall take steps to ensure that only persons adequately qualified are appointed traffic wardens, and that traffic wardens *are suitably trained before undertaking their duties.* s. 81(5) RTRA 1967.

There is a military ring about 'training', but traffic wardens are not unlike soldiers in that they are an auxiliary force, recruited to release the professional for more active duty. No disrespect is intended by way of comparison with the early Local Defence Volunteers, subsequently formed into the Home Guard and caricatured in 'Dad's Army'. Before 1960 there were strong rumours from the North of posses of civilian police aides or vigilantes formed on the lines of Popski's Private Army. This could not be tolerated, hence the provision insisted upon by the Police Federation in 1960—not

117

that *retired* police constables might not be recruited (as indeed they are).

Traffic wardens may be civilians but they are no Dad's Army. They may not as yet be able to agree on a Rule Book, but they understand police discipline. Their training may vary from the highly sophisticated computer-controlled areas to the lone country beat but the courses have all to be Home Office approved. The following is a provincial specimen. (Metropolitan courses are naturally longer and tougher).

First Day:
> Introduction to the Department.
> Conditions of Service.
> Appointment and Employment of Traffic Wardens, Section 81—R.T.R. Act 1967.
> Functions of Traffic Wardens Order 1970.

Second and Third Days:
> Introduction to and Instruction on—
> The Controlled Parking Zone,
> The Parking Meter,
> The Fixed Penalty System,
> Facilities for Disabled Drivers,
> Exemptions permitted at Parking Places and in Restricted Streets.

Fourth Day:
> Instruction on—
> Traffic Control and the Highway Code,
> Legislation relating to—
> Pedestrian Crossings,
> Removal of vehicles.
> Guidance on giving evidence in Court.
> Procedures for handling Lost and Found Property.

Second and Third Week:
> The Traffic Warden recruit performs Street Duty under the supervision of an experienced Traffic Warden, receiving guidance in the enforcement of Traffic Regulations, manner of dealing with members of the public and practical experience in traffic control.

A course of three weeks is average. In London the course may be up to four weeks. The London recruitment brochure points out that this is only the formal, classroom, training. The real training begins on the street. An experienced warden will accompany the novice. She will 'break you in gently'. —*You are not thrown in the deep end*—among the sharks basking on yellow lines?

A point which may puzzle the parking offender is how a traffic warden can memorise every case, as she must in the event of a prosecution. In the metropolis this is achieved with the aid of the modern computer programmed ticket, the FPN Mark 2 which is on general issue in areas which employ the computer. Every essential fact is recorded, the class of vehicle, any foreign registration, whether the driver was seen at the time or later, yellow lines and kerb markings, licensing authority, the warden's special area, whether constant or casual observation was kept, valve position unaltered, loading or unloading seen or not seen, position of time plate, if any, restrictions and precise position of vehicle. There is space for what the driver said, not omitting expletives, and for the name and address given. (M Mouse, Fla, is not acceptable).

The course will include a visit to the office where tickets are processed, the Central Ticket Office where spent tickets are fed to the computer. Some offices keep a Black Museum where the recruit is shown the shambles likely to result from a mistake. Wardens are all instructed that the FPN is the warden's best friend but it does need careful handling. The FPN Mark 2 is not foolproof. It can backfire.

What goes into the warden's sack is naturally a secret. There is of course her Pocket Book, the hourly record of her movements open to the supervisor's inspection. What she carries in addition to her ammunition is a matter of personal choice. A spare ballpoint, certainly, a roll of Sellotape, perhaps a torch for winter evenings, a compass to get her bearings right, a footrule possibly, a magnifying glass and her reading glasses. A street directory is not encouraged. She must not be delayed answering tourist's questions. She needs to know only her own beat. She must of course know the right time and watches will have been synchronized before she sets out. A stopped watch can be an embarrassment but watches are not a free issue. She may have a bleeper, but she's unlikely to get a police whistle. Unarmed combat is not on the syllabus. She will need pennies, for nature's call and to call her unit, or the removal squad. She will not have change for parking meters.

Training never stops for the traffic warden. There are constant refresher courses, new tricks to be learnt. So it is for the motorist. He must train to become his own warden. If you can't beat them . . .

Traffic Wardens: Uniform

The traffic warden out of uniform is positively naked. The law is very firm on this point.

> Traffic wardens shall wear such uniform as the Secretary of State may determine, and shall not act as traffic wardens when not in uniform. (s 81(6) RTRA 1967).

It is this need at all times to be in uniform that sets the traffic warden apart. When dealing with the parking offender or his vehicle the traffic warden has the same powers as the police but if he is not in uniform he cannot act. Not so the police, whose powers are not limited unless the law specifically requires the constable to be 'in uniform,' eg to require a roadside breath test or to prosecute a jaywalker who disobeys his traffic regulation.

The Home Office 'determined' from the outset that the uniform of the warden should be conspicuous, hence the prominent use of yellow, the colour chosen by the AA with no political bias since 1905 and sanctioned in 1964 by the Worboys Report on traffic signs. Yellow is the colour of the roadmarking for the No Waiting street. It was singularly appropriate for the traffic warden and if it earned him the nickname of 'wasp', that too was appropriate. The wasps were attracted to traffic jams and had no scruples about stinging parking offenders. It is the headgear with the yellow band that distinguishes the traffic warden.

The uniform suits the younger, slim figure. It does not suit so well the middle-aged or corpulent. A senior lecturer in sociology writing for *New Society* has mentioned the uniform as among the several factors which 'help the warden to be seen as an embodiment of authoritarianism':

> His title—warden—has unfortunate connotations, for a start. Some of the footwear worn by the women wardens resembles jackboots, especially if the wearer has a matronly build. One magistrate is on record as having referred to a warden as a 'Belsen wardress'.

This sociologist was studying the traffic warden in Manchester, and it does seem that in the North the traffic warden is built more heavily. In the South they do appear to be lighter. The uniform is such an important feature in recruiting that a decision has been taken in the Metropolitan force for a new costume. This has been designed at the London College of Fashion and is to consist of an A-line skirt, a longer jacket, a bow tie and a smaller and neater hat. This only follows the pattern set long ago at Chester where the elegant wife of the Chief Constable went to her own couturier, Worth, for the design.

The traffic warden service has no CID or plain clothes branch. Keeping observation to detect meter feeding is left to police or to municipal attendants who require no uniform. Wardens do however spare their clients' feelings on 'follow up' duties, chasing the unpaid ticket. Many conceal the uniform and when at one time the Metropolitan force allowed wardens to accept payment of overdue tickets an identity card was issued. The practice has been discontinued in London but it may be permitted elsewhere. And at car pounds there is already sufficient 'aggro', so that wardens may temporarily discard the hat while they collect the removal fee. But otherwise the rule is that on duty the full uniform must be worn.

Traffic Wardens: Witness Statements
Our ticket system deals only with 'self-proving' offences. The very fact of the vehicle waiting in a restricted street provides a

case to answer. If the driver, or the owner, refuses the opportunity to settle out of court there must be a prosecution, leading to a hearing before the magistrates. There can be no short-circuit of court procedure. The prosecution must prove its case. The traffic warden is the star witness. If the warden does not go into the witness box the prosecution must fail.

Prosecutors—the officers at ticket offices—know very well the understandable fears which many wardens have of giving evidence. Traffic wardens with cold feet are known to be no longer available when required to attend court. After six months and a hundred intervening cases the mind goes blank when asked to remember details which may be etched for ever on the mind of the defendant. The courtroom spins as all wait for the answer to questions put by the sharp young counsel who has cut his teeth on the ticket and is prepared to set the summons to music. It is an ordeal, giving evidence. As for recognizing the defendant, this after so long is impossible. The warden lies awake, worrying. Will she do herself justice?

But not to worry. The computer will sort out the evidence, provided the ticket counterfoil is properly marked to be programmed. Even with no such aid the prosecutor will prepare the warden's statement and will serve it upon the defendant. This will be read out in court unless the defendant insists upon the attendance of the witness. Few avail themselves of their right. (Section 9 Criminal Justice Act 1967).

The following is the witness statement of a traffic warden, a girl of 19. The facts were not disputed but the defendant, a doctor-resident, claimed the need to park near his home since he needed to load and unload a case of medical instruments. He pleaded Not Guilty and was granted an Absolute Discharge with only a token order of costs.

On 31st December at 0830 hours I saw a motor vehicle stationary in Prince of Wales Drive, S.W.11 where there is a statutory restriction on waiting by vehicles. I kept constant observation on the vehicle until 0835 hours and saw no loading or unloading taking place. At all times during the period of observation I was in a good position to see any such activity.

There was a time plate which applied to waiting on that day beside the vehicle showing waiting restrictions from 0800 hours to 1830 hours.

The vehicle was parked on a single yellow line by the south kerb facing west, outside No. 1.

I saw the driver who reached his car door as I had just finished the Fixed Penalty Notice. I said 'You are too late. I have already done the ticket'. He just shrugged his shoulders, got in the car and drove off.

The traffic warden in Britain must envy her opposite number in the United States. The traffic warden in Philadelphia, for example, signs the following statement on the ticket.

The undersigned further states that he has just and reasonable grounds to believe and does believe, that the person named above is committing the offence set forth, contrary to law and that a copy of this summons and complaint has been served upon said person as required by law.

There is space for signature of officer and badge number and for it to be 'sworn to and subscribed before me this date, signature of judge.' This is enough for a conviction.

Yellow Lines

Our system of single and double yellow lines was first introduced in the late 1950s. It was the result not only of environmental objection to upright No Waiting signs, but because of the difficulty in delineating precisely where restrictions applied. No system can be entirely free from abuse but our system presents few problems. It works well and it allows traffic wardens a measure of discretion. We are now asked to consider whether our sophisticated system should not be altered to conform to the crude European standard of a single yellow line to indicate 'no stopping' and a single broken yellow line to indicate 'no waiting'. Consultations continue. There will certainly be no change overnight.

Most of us well understand the general meaning of a yellow line. It means No Waiting, except for limited loading and

unloading. A single continuous yellow line means no waiting for at least 8 hours between 7 am and 7 pm on 4 or more days of the week. This usually means 'the working day' but it can include Sundays. The restriction applies to the whole of the carriageway including the footway and verges. It extends normally from building line to building line. Double yellow lines indicate the same restriction *plus* some additional period between 7 pm and 7 am. Broken yellow lines indicate any other restriction.

In addition to the yellow lines there are normally small yellow time plates erected at the roadside, facing the carriageway, at recommended 200 foot intervals. These give more precise details than the general indication given by the yellow lines. Yellow plates are not however required in controlled zones—those areas where on-street parking is authorized, as at parking meters, where the hours of operation are shown on the zone entry signs. Where restrictions vary within a con-controlled zone time plates are required. (Loading restrictions —the term covers also unloading—are marked by yellow kerb markings ('blips' or chevrons) and time plates. This is similar to the yellow line system, with one, two or three 'blips' according to the hours of operation).

Yellow lines need constant maintenance. Yellow lines, like old soldiers, do tend to fade away. As Mr Muddlecombe JP might say, 'The quality of paint used on our roads is a national disgrace. Case dismissed'. And he would be right. No yellow line, no offence, unless it be for causing obstruction. This was demonstrated at Cardiff Crown Court only recently when His Honour Judge Hywel ap Robert allowed an appeal from a conviction for waiting in a restricted street on an ancient gap in a yellow line. The gap, measuring 15 feet, had been allowed to remain over a period of six months. The learned judge looked to Scotland for his authority—Macleod v Hamilton 1965 SLT 305—and decided he should follow the fair prin-ciple that restriction orders must be made known to the public by the forms of traffic signs prescribed. 'Though the appellant himself realized that parking restrictions were intended to be in force, cases of this kind cannot depend on the state of mind of individual road users'. (Goode v Hayward, reported in September 1976 *Criminal Law Review*). Borough Engineers must really sit up and take notice of this decision. Ministry instructions are quite explicit:

Signs must at all times be maintained to preserve their original effectiveness and general condition. *It is a waste of public money to provide signs only to allow them to lose their effectiveness by subsequent deterioration.*

As for meter zones there is a 1975 Direction in the Traffic Signs Regulations which now requires all parts of a controlled zone not allocated to parking bays to be marked with yellow lines. This should get over the decision that London is peculiar in not requiring yellow lines. (Cooper v Hall 1968 1 WLR 360).

Yellow lines act as a deterrent but you must not be tempted to take the law into your own hands. There was the case of the man who rang up the Town Hall and was told where he could buy yellow plastic paint. He lined the entrance to his garage and it worked very well until the would-be parker turned out to be the Borough Surveyor. His offence was under the Highways (Miscellaneous Provisions) Act 1961 for which there can be a fine up to £100.

If a person without lawful authority or excuse . . . paints or otherwise inscribes or affixes upon the surfaces of a highway, or upon any structure or works on or in a highway, any picture, letter, sign or other mark . . . he shall be guilty of an offence.

'Polite Notice—No Parking' is *not* approved.

STUDIES IN BRITISH TRANSPORT HISTORY 1870–1970
Derek H Aldcroft
£6.75

A Professor of Economic History presents the economic aspects of
Britain's transport history. Topics include: railways and economic
growth; British shipping and foreign competition – the Anglo-German
rivalry; the depression in British shipping; the decontrol of the shipping
and railways after World War I; the eclipse of the coastal shipping
trade; port congestion and the shipping boom; the restriction of road
passenger transport; Britain's internal airways; railways and air transport;
innovation on the railways; the changing pattern of demand; reflections
on the Rochdale Inquiry.

SENSIBLE DRIVING
The Logical Basis of Everyday Motoring
M J Hosken
£3.25   18 illustrations

Filling the gap between primers and specialist volumes, this book is
intended for the driver who has passed the driving test but who knows
there is still a great deal to be learnt about the art of good driving.
From construction and use of the car to braking, cornering and motorway driving, country lanes and parking – Michael Hosken covers the
whole spectrum of road situations.

ROADS AND THEIR TRAFFIC 1750–1850
John Copeland
£4.50   16pp illustrations

A description of the roads as they were maintained by the statute labour
of the parishes, and the improvements made to them by the growing
number of turnpike trusts. Chapters include: the roads in the mid-18th
century; road improvements 1750–1850; the carriage of goods; the
carriage of passengers; the carriage of mail; travelling style; the first
generation of steam carriages; competition with the railways.

AUTOMOBILE DESIGN: GREAT DESIGNERS AND THEIR WORK
(Eds) Ronald Barket and Anthony Harding
£4.75   DCP £3.25   109 illustrations

The biographies of 11 pioneering automobile engineers with emphasis
on their design work and achievements. The Bollees, Frederick
Lanchester, Henry M Leland, Hans Ledwinka, Marc Birkigt, Ferdinand
Porsche, Harry Miller, Vittorio Jano, Gabriel Voisin, Alec Issigonis and
Colin Chapman.

A HISTORY OF THE LONDON TAXICAB
G N Georgano
£3.75 31 illustrations

The development of the taxicab from the hackney-coach to present day motor cabs and minicabs. Contents: hackney coach to hansom cab; 'Umming Birds and Mortar Carts'; the arrival of the motor cab; owners, drivers and public; taxicabs between the wars; four seats good, two seats bad; the post-war taxicab; Michael Gotla's private army; taxicabs today and tomorrow.

THE LAND-ROVER
Work Horse of the World
Graham Robson
£4.95 43 illustrations

Here is the first complete history of a remarkable vehicle published in the year when the millionth vehicle comes off the assembly line. Conceived as a stop-gap to help its manufacturers through post-war austerity and shortage of materials, within two years it had become the company's mainstay. Graham Robson chronicles all the prototypes, projects and special models including developments made for the armed services and the luxurious range rover.

LEARNER DRIVER
Joe Kells
£3.50 line illustrations

Intended primarily for the novice motorist under instruction, this book examines in clear and straightforward style the problems of learning to drive a motor vehicle and of attaining as quickly as possible the necessary proficiency to pass the official Driving Test. Much helpful advice is given on the variety of situations likely to be encountered in everyday driving and the reader is forewarned of what to expect in the Driving Test itself. An additional chapter on 'How a Car Works' provides a simplified explanation of the main components.

BRITISH TRANSPORT SINCE 1914
An Economic History
Derek H Aldcroft
£12.50 13 illustrations

This book provides an up-to-date survey of developments in the main sectors of British transport since 1914. Attention is focused particularly on the trends since World War I and the author discusses the problems created by the rapid changes in the structure of transport demand and shifts in technology. It covers virtually all forms of transport, including infrastructures, and it is the first comprehensive survey to be published.